EARLY YEARS ACTIVITY CHEST

Struc
play

CW00417986

CREDITS

British Library Cataloguing-in-Publication Data
A catalogue record for this book is available from the British Library.

ISBN 0 439 98440 8

AUTHOR
Linda Mort

EDITOR
Jane Bishop

ASSISTANT EDITOR
Lesley Sudlow

SERIES DESIGNER
Lynne Joesbury

DESIGNER
Catherine Mason

ILLUSTRATIONS
Julie Clough

COVER PHOTOGRAPH
Martyn Chillmaid

Text © 2003 Linda Mort
© 2003 Scholastic Ltd
Designed using Adobe Pagemaker
Published by Scholastic Ltd, Villiers House,
Clarendon Avenue, Leamington Spa, Warwickshire CV32 5PR
Printed by Alden Group Ltd, Oxford
Visit our website at www.scholastic.co.uk

1 2 3 4 5 6 7 8 9 0   3 4 5 6 7 8 9 0 1 2

CONTENTS

CONTENTS

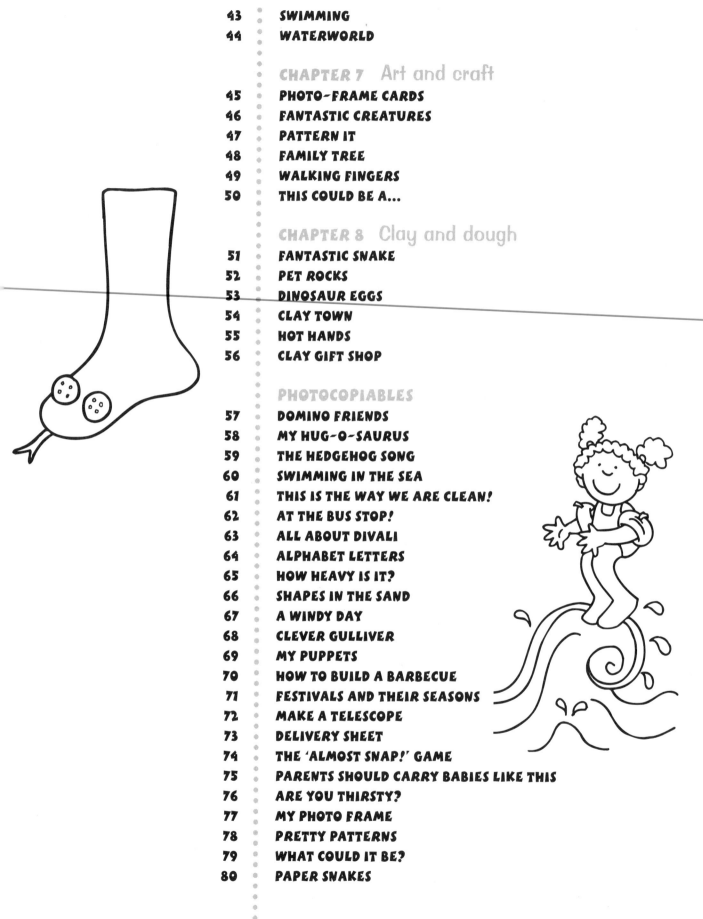

Introduction

The aims of the series

This book is one of a series that aims to provide enjoyable and practical dip-in activities for children aged three to five. The activities will develop and extend young children's learning across all areas of the curriculum, in accordance with the Early Learning Goals of the *Curriculum Guidance for the Foundation Stage* (QCA), and the documents on pre-school education published for Scotland, Wales and Northern Ireland.

What is structured play?

Structured play is the name that is given to play experiences in which an adult is present with children as they play. The adult acts as a role model, to initiate, develop and extend the children's learning. The role of the adult, in providing structured play experiences, is to plan for a specific learning outcome, to prepare the environment in terms of appropriate space, time and resources, to interact with the children and to record and evaluate the learning. As with all kinds of play experiences, structured play is at its most successful when it is carefully matched with children's developmental needs and current interests.

Children have an innate motivation to imitate their parents, carers and older siblings. This powerful motivation engages them at every level – physically, emotionally, socially and intellectually – as they learn to make sense of the world. Adults who actively engage in helping children to replicate behaviour, greatly develop children's capacity for learning. This natural process is seen at its most obvious level in babyhood, when an adult smiles and the baby imitates. The adult responds by repeating the smile, as does the baby, and the learning is reinforced. Learning has fully taken place when the baby can smile independently, and at will.

Structured play can be described as an extension of children's natural learning pattern in the home environment. It is universally accepted that parents and carers are the children's first teachers. Children are born imitators of adults' body language, gestures, mannerisms, speech and actions.

During role-play, children experiment with new behaviours, then assimilate them, and apply them in different situations. Structured play offers early years practitioners a very effective way of developing children's learning, which is in tune with their needs and holistic patterns of learning.

The three-part cycle

It is helpful to think of structured play activities in terms of a three-part cycle.

1 Ideally, the learning potential of structured play activities is enhanced, if the activities can be introduced by some kind of memorable and engaging first-hand experience.

2 Learning is supported and maintained through a second stage, in which the adult models related play experiences, using appropriate vocabulary to develop conceptual understanding.

3 In the third stage, the provision of play equipment and resources can encourage children to assimilate and 'take ownership' of the previous experiences by, for example, playing productively in groups of children, including 'playing at teacher', or creating their own pictures, models and constructions and so on, without the direct input of an adult all of the time.

1   Introducing structured play

Children's learning at home always takes place in the context of the powerfully motivating force of the presence of loved adults, doing real things in the real world. It is important for early years practitioners to try to introduce structured play activities in inventive ways in order to capture the children's interest and imagination. Such 'introductions' convey to children the message that what is to follow will be as interesting and as important as events at home.

Parents, carers and other visitors who introduce activities are obviously very valuable in this context. An introduction that contains an element of surprise can also serve to help children make connections in their learning. For example, in the activity 'Garden I Spy' on page 34, it is suggested that the practitioner hang a ladle from a tree. A child may have seen one at home, but not yet learned its name. Seeing one on a tree is intriguing, and helps the child to be receptive to new learning, such as remembering the word or learning its initial sound.

2   Modelling behaviour

During the second stage of the cycle, it is highly beneficial to provide many real props, dressing-up clothes and examples of environmental print, as appropriate, in order to maintain the children's motivation to master 'real' situations, for example, the 'hospital', 'post office', or 'hairdresser's'.

When the adult is acting as a role model and models behaviour for the children, it is important for the practitioner then to try not to dominate and stifle the children's play by being too prescriptive. The adult should introduce an idea, new words or technique, then try to stand back as soon as the children begin to develop competence, but be on hand to support and, when appropriate, develop the play.

This sensitive interaction between the children and the practitioner makes for productive play at an appropriate level of challenge.

3 Consolidating learning

In the third stage of a structured play activity, the practitioner should carefully prepare the environment in such a way as to prompt the children to indirectly recall their learning from the first and second stages. This is an ideal opportunity for a practitioner to assess, through observation, how much a child has learned by, for example, listening to whether a child uses any words encountered previously, or tries to use a recently introduced technique in a practical activity. For example, in the activity 'This could be a...' on page 50, the children are introduced to, and practise the activity of, imagining what a shape could be, by adding drawn details on paper, with the support of the practitioner.

On other occasions, the activity suggests that the practitioner leave out, in the art area, prepared sheets of plain paper, with a torn piece of tissue paper stuck in the centre. By observing what the children do, independently, the practitioner can assess their level of recall of previous learning and ability to explore, creatively, shapes in two dimensions.

How to use this book

Each chapter in the book is based on a familiar play area of early years settings: Role-play; Sand; Small-world; Construction; Outdoor play and Natural discovery; Water; Art and craft and Clay and dough. Within each chapter there are six ideas, one to cover each Area of Learning: Personal, social and emotional development; Communication, language and literacy; Mathematical development; Knowledge and understanding of the world; Physical development and Creative development.

An optimum group size and an approximate duration is suggested for each activity, as well as lists for what is required, with details of any necessary preparation and an easy-to-follow description of how to carry it out. The rate at which children develop varies, but, in general, the activities are aimed at four-year-olds, with support ideas for three-year-olds and extension ideas for five-year-olds. Every activity includes suggestions for 'home links' and many include suggestions for adding a multicultural dimension.

How to use the photocopiable pages

The photocopiable pages are aimed at children of four years and above. Each one is related to an activity in the book. The pages are headed with child-friendly instructions and can be sent home as a useful prompt for family discussion, or kept in a child's portfolio as evidence of learning experiences and progress.

Using a wide variety of resources

The 'What you need' section of each activity lists suggestions for what is required. Only items that are readily available in any setting, or that are easily obtainable, are listed. Many structured play activities benefit by being introduced to children in a striking and memorable way, in order to capture their attention and fully engage their imagination and concentration. For this reason, the 'What you need' section sometimes begins with suggestions for bringing in real items, which can be easily borrowed from practitioners', parents' or carers' homes.

Links with home

Children's learning is developed every time that they are enabled to make connections in their learning between one context and another, hence the importance of links with home. The suggested 'Home links' ideas in the book are a way of following up the children's learning in the home environment. Many activities suggest that the home activity be displayed or recognised in some way, when they are brought back to the setting. This process provides a useful opportunity for practitioners and families to chat about a child's recall of, and reaction to, the learning experiences provided in the setting. In addition, children's self-esteem is enhanced, and their learning reinforced, when, for example, they bring back a section of a 'snake' decorated at home as part of an assignment initiated at the setting the previous day (see the activity 'Fantastic snake' on page 51). Practitioners must always, of course, exercise discretion and sensitivity concerning children's home circumstances.

Structured play activities provide many opportunities for inviting parents and carers into the setting to give a short talk, ideally with a simple demonstration, about an aspect of their occupation or hobby. They provide the ideal, memorable and motivating introductory phase to a structured play experience. Such visits are particularly relevant concerning multicultural experiences; however, practitioners should be confident, before asking, that the parent or carer approached, for example, to talk about a festival, would be happy to do so.

Multicultural links

Some of the activities suggest ways to ensure that the cultural diversity of our society is used to enhance the children's work. These ideas include saying words in different languages and telling multicultural stories, as well as finding out about traditions in other countries.

CHAPTER 1

Use role-play to stimulate the children's imaginations, raise awareness of the needs and feelings of other people and to reinforce learning in a wide range of areas.

Role-play

GROUP SIZE
Four children.

TIMING
Ten minutes.

GETTING USED TO IT

Learning objective
To have a developing awareness of their own needs, views and feelings and be sensitive to the needs, views and feelings of others. (Personal, social and emotional development)

What you need
A paper plate; felt-tipped pens; small piece of white card; split-pin fastener; scissors; dolls; teddy bears; four trays; jigsaw or construction items.

Preparation
Draw hair, eyebrows, eyes and a nose on the paper plate. Draw and cut out a curved mouth on the small piece of card and attach it to the paper plate with the split-pin fastener.

What to do
Explain to the children that when new children start at the setting they have to be helped to settle in and 'get used to it'. Move the mouth on the paper plate to look sad, and explain that sometimes new children feel sad when they first say goodbye to their parents or carers. Say that we can help them to cheer up and feel happy again by showing them lots of interesting things to do. Move the mouth to show a happy expression. Invite the children to talk about their memories of settling in.

Ask each child to choose a doll or teddy to help settle in. Let each child choose a table-top activity that they think their doll or teddy would enjoy. Give each child a tray and ask them to bring back, for example, a jigsaw, some DUPLO bricks or Constructo straws. Sit the children in a circle on the floor with their dolls or teddies and trays and encourage them to talk to their doll or teddy about what they are doing. Ask the children from time to time about how they think their doll or teddy is feeling.

HOME LINKS
Let the children make a simple card and lolly-stick puppet to take home. Ask each child to settle in their puppet at home by explaining to them how to use their toys and games.

Support
Let younger children show their doll or teddy what they are doing, as you provide a commentary.

Extension
Ask older children to each choose a glove puppet and explain how to do something, for the puppet to try, for example, build a tower of bricks, shake a maraca or hold a pencil.

GROUP SIZE
Six children.

TIMING
15 minutes.

'PLEASE AND THANK YOU' HOUSE

Learning objective

To speak clearly and with confidence and control and to show awareness of the listener, for example, by use of greetings such as, 'please' and 'thank you'. (Communication, language and literacy)

What you need

Four free-standing poles (such as from an outdoor traffic-sign set); piece of light material; small table; seven chairs; two small food items (banana slices and satsuma segments); two plates; knife; two wood blocks.

Preparation

Drape the material over the poles to make a roof. Arrange two chairs and a table in the 'house'. Place the remaining five chairs in a row opposite the house.

What to do

Put the banana slices and satsuma segments on two plates. Explain the importance of saying 'please' and 'thank you' when receiving, or being offered, something. Say that people are allowed into the 'please and thank you' house only if they can use these words.

Sit in the house yourself and ask one child to hold the wood blocks and stand outside the house. Ask the remaining five children to sit on the chairs. Invite the first 'visitor' to pretend to knock on the door, as the child with the wood blocks plays them. Say, 'Hello, (child's name), please sit down. Would you like some banana or satsuma?'.

Remind the child to say, 'Banana, please' or, 'Satsuma,

please', and then, 'Thank you', just before they eat. Then say, 'Goodbye, (child's name), and thank you for coming.'

When each child has been a visitor, let them take turns to be the host or hostess. Later in the session, or the following day, serve the same two food items at snack time, to jog the children's memories about saying 'please' and 'thank you'. Note who does so spontaneously.

Support

Let younger children just take on the visitor role in the 'please and thank you' house.

Extension

Talk with older children about their experiences of saying 'please' and 'thank you' concerning kind behaviour, for example, when helping or comforting one another.

HOME LINKS
Ask parents and carers to tell you about their children saying 'please' and 'thank you'.

MULTICULTURAL LINKS
Let the children make a poster with speech bubbles featuring the words 'please' and 'thank you' in various languages.

WHAT NUMBER BUS?

Learning objective
To recognise numerals 1 to 9. (Mathematical development)

What you need
Four copies of the photocopiable sheet on page 62; crayons; laminator; four small-world people; tray; four toy cars; two pieces of A4 card; wipeable markers; scissors; sticky tape; drawstring bag.

Preparation
Colour in each photocopiable sheet and laminate them. Cut four strips from one piece of card, approximately two centimetres in depth, and stick one around each car, to make a bus. Write a number on the front of each and ask the children to draw windows on each bus. Put the buses on the 'bus station' tray. Cut the second piece of card into four rectangles and write a number on each one. Draw a row of dots corresponding to the number on each card.

What to do
If possible, take the children to look at a nearby bus stop. Talk about the numbers on the stop, for example, 'A four and a two side by side means number 42. The number 42 bus goes to the station'.

Back inside, sit the children around a table and show them the buses on the 'bus station' tray. Give each child a laminated sheet and a wipeable marker and ask them to write the numbers of the buses on their bus stop.

Invite each child to choose a small-world person and stand it at the bus stop on their sheet. Ask them to choose a 'destination' and tell them the number of the bus that 'goes to that place'.

Put the cards in the bag, and invite the first child to choose one. If the card matches their bus number, they can take a bus from the tray, move it along the road at the bottom of their sheet to their bus stop, and sit their small-world person on it.

Encourage the children to keep their bus at their bus stop and to pass the bag to the next child, who chooses a card and, if it matches, can move a bus to their bus stop.

Continue passing the bag around, until the winning child moves their bus from their stop to their destination.

Support
Use only two numbers with younger children.

Extension
Omit the dots on the cards for older children

GROUP SIZE
Up to six children.

TIMING
Ten minutes.

HOME LINKS
Make coconut barfi with the children and send home the following recipe:

Coconut barfi

Ingredients
175g evaporated milk; 150g desiccated coconut; 100g golden granulated sugar

Method
Pour the milk into a saucepan. Add the sugar and heat on a low flame. Stir from time to time. Bring gently to the boil and simmer until the milk has reduced by half. Add half of the coconut, stir for five minutes, then add the rest of the coconut. Grease a toffee tray and spread the barfi on it. Leave to cool and cut into cubes.

DIVALI CIRCLE

Learning objective
To begin to know about their own cultures and beliefs and those of other people. (Knowledge and understanding of the world)

What you need
A4- and A5-sized copies of the photocopiable sheet on page 63; scissors; lidded shoebox; sheet of brightly-coloured sugar paper; sticky tape; percussion instrument or CD player or tape recorder and CD or cassette tape of Asian music.

Preparation
Cover the shoebox and lid with the sugar paper, securing with sticky tape. Cut out the pictures from the photocopiable sheets.

What to do
Invite a parent or carer to talk about how Divali is celebrated, for example, by cleaning the house, making cards, painting mendhi patterns on hands, making clay divas, rangoli floor patterns and special foods, such as coconut barfi. Arrange for the children to be involved in some or all of the activities illustrated on the sheet. Sit the children in a circle and hold up, and talk about, the enlarged pictures.

Put the smaller pictures in the shoebox and give it to a child to hold. Play the instrument or music and ask the child to pass the box around the circle, until you stop playing. Ask the child holding the box to take out a picture and, not letting anyone else see it, to mime the actions for the other children to guess. Continue until everyone has had a turn.

Support
Let younger children show their picture to the rest of the circle, and ask everyone to join in the actions of the mime.

Extension
Give older children a copy each of the photocopiable sheet and ask them to put the pictures together in a book called 'All about Divali'.

GROUP SIZE
Up to four children.

TIMING
Approximately 15 minutes.

CAR MECHANICS

Learning objective
To handle tools, objects, construction and malleable materials safely and with increasing control. (Physical development)

What you need
Wooden and plastic construction and tool sets (such as Big Builder or Briomec); small, lightweight 'sit-and-ride' car; large plastic nut and bolt; parcel tape; two tables; strong string.

Preparation
Turn the 'sit-and-ride' car upside-down and stick the bolt to the underside in an easily accessible place, using parcel tape. Put the tables either side of the car. Lift the car up so that the top is flush with the table-tops, and tie it tightly on all sides to the table legs with string so that it cannot wobble or fall.

What to do
Explain to the children that when cars have to be repaired, a mechanic sometimes has to lie underneath it, in the 'car workshop', while the car is lifted up on a 'ramp'.

Give three children (the mechanics) various pieces of construction sets (engine parts) to work on individually, while the fourth mechanic lies down, face upwards, underneath the ramp, with a nut which must be screwed back into place on the bolt, on the underside of the car. When this has been done, another mechanic may have a turn.

Support
Stick the bolt to the upper shell of the car, for example, in the boot, so that younger children can stand up instead of lying down to screw the nut on the bolt.

Extension
Encourage older children to take turns to role-play one child being the mechanic and the other a customer whose car needs to be fixed (using the nut and bolt).

HOME LINKS
Put a sign on the door saying that if parents and carers are having a car repaired or serviced, could they tell their children something about it, so that the children can tell everyone in the setting.

GROUP SIZE
Six children.

TIMING
About 15 minutes.

ABRACADABRA!

Learning objective

To use their imagination in art and design, music, dance, imaginative and role-play and stories. (Creative development)

What you need

A copy of the story of 'Cinderella' (Traditional); a sheet of white A3 paper; black felt-tipped pen; orange crayon; a double-page spread from a magazine; tin foil; tinsel or foil parcel 'rosette'; sticky tape; 'magic' hat and cape.

Preparation

Make a 'magic wand' by rolling the magazine pages diagonally into a tight cylinder and securing with sticky tape. Cover with foil and stick tinsel or a rosette at the top with the sticky tape. Draw a large pumpkin on the white paper and colour it orange.

What to do

Talk about the fairy godmother in Cinderella and show a picture of her with her magic wand and pumpkin. Explain that there are many stories about fairies, magicians, sorcerers, wizards and other people who can do magic spells, and that it is fun to pretend to be them. Tell the children that they can take turns to pretend to be a magic person and turn a friend into an animal and back again.

Invite the first child to put on the 'magic' hat and cape, wave the magic wand at another child and say, 'Abracadabra! I am turning you into a cat chasing a ball of wool,' (or a dog burying a bone, or a monkey climbing a tree and so on). The second child must carry out the actions, making any appropriate sound effects. Then ask the 'magician' to turn the animal back into a child again. Let the children change roles.

Some children may like to think of alternative magic words or phrases, besides 'Abracadabra', and to devise a sequence of actions in addition to waving the magic wand, for example, waving the wand three times, stamping four times, or twirling around twice.

Support

Let younger children see two or three toy animals, to help them 'make a spell', and encourage them to simply say, 'Abracadabra! You are a...!'.

Extension

Encourage older children to think of ingredients for a magic potion, and use emergent writing skills to write the recipe on paper. Staple them together to make a 'Book of magic'.

HOME LINKS
Let the children make a magic wand to take home to turn their family members into animals!

CHAPTER 2

Sand

Use sand play to encourage the children to work together, explore letter-writing and experiment with a programmable toy.

Four children.

Ten minutes.

HOW MANY SCOOPS?

Learning objective
To work as part of a group or class, taking turns and sharing fairly. (Personal, social and emotional development)

What you need
A sand tray of damp sand; chair for each child and the adult; ice-cream scoop; five plastic plates; label from a carton of chocolate ice-cream.

Preparation
Ask the children to sit around the sand tray and to smooth the sand.

What to do
Show the children the ice-cream label and tell them about a giant called Grizzlegrub, who ate a whole carton of chocolate ice-cream by himself without sharing it. Say that afterwards he felt greedy because he had eaten it all alone, and that he also began to feel sick. Tell the children that next time he shared the ice-cream with his friends, using an ice-cream scoop, which was great fun, and that he did not feel sick.

Encourage the children to pretend to be Grizzlegrub sharing out the 'chocolate ice-cream' sand. Give everyone a plate, including yourself, and invite a child to be Grizzlegrub. Encourage them to ask everyone how many scoops of ice-cream (sand) they would like, and to give them the correct number. Later, put the ice-cream scoop in the home corner for the children to use to share out imaginary ice-cream.

Support
For younger children, cut out a paper circle for each plate. Draw up to four small scoop-sized circles on each piece of paper. Encourage the children to count their circles by touching them one at a time, and to ask for the same number of scoops.

Extension
With older children, use the game to practice in oral addition and subtraction. After each child has received their scoops, ask if they would like some more. When they have received more, ask how many scoops they have altogether. For subtraction practice, give each child a spoon with which to pretend to eat a scoopful, and then ask how many scoops they have left.

At the end of the session, invite each child to demonstrate to their parent or carer how they can use a scoop. Suggest that the child could use one at home for enjoyable counting practice.

Let the children use a scoop to share out ice-cream desserts from other countries, such as Kulfi from India and Bastani from Iran.

HOME LINKS
Write each child's name on a piece of sandpaper, using a thick, black wax crayon. Indicate the starting-point for each letter with a dot of red wax crayon. Ask each child to stroke the letters, using their forefinger, and verbalising how they form each one. Write each child's name on paper, using the same size of lettering, and starting dots. Ask each child to write on top of your writing. Put a starting dot underneath each letter and ask each child to try copying the letters. Send home the sandpaper 'tickly names' for practice.

MULTICULTURAL LINKS
Make enlarged, laminated versions of letter shapes of other alphabet scripts, asking parents and carers for advice on letter formation families and order of presentation.

LETTER SANDBOXES

Learning objective

To learn to write alphabet letters, using the correct formation. (Communication, language and literacy)

What you need

Four plastic seed trays (without holes), approximately 36cm x 24cm; damp sand; four dried-up ballpoint pens; copy of the photocopiable sheet on page 64; laminator.

Preparation

Enlarge the photocopiable sheet for each child and laminate them Ask the children to help fill the trays with damp sand.

What to do

Give each child a seed tray and a laminated photocopiable sheet. Talk about how, when we write alphabet letters, it is a good idea to try to remember which 'family' the letter belongs to, such as the 'straight-line family', the 'curvy family', the 'roundy family' or the 'down-up family'. Hold up your sheet and trace over the letters of the 'straight-line family', telling the children the sound of each letter, and verbalising your finger movements, for example, 'This letter has the sound "w" and my finger goes down, up, down, up'. Repeat, asking the children to trace over the letters with their fingers.

Give each child a dried-up pen, remind them how to hold it properly, and ask them to 'write' over the letters again, using the pen. Ask the children to copy the letters in the trays, first using their fingers, and then their pens.

Support

Concentrate on one or two letters at a time with younger children.

Extension

Ask older children to use their name cards to copy their names in the sand, using fingers or pens, and to fill in the letter shapes with small stones or shells.

GROUP SIZE
Four children.

TIMING
Ten minutes.

GOING DOWN A BIT

Learning objective

To use the terms 'more', 'less', 'heavier' and 'lighter'. (Mathematical development)

What you need

A set of balancing scales; eight small, transparent plastic sandwich bags with ties; dry sand; small sand scoop; four copies of the photocopiable sheet on page 65.

Preparation

Half fill the bags with the same amount of sand, using the scoop. Wind a tie around the top of each bag.

What to do

Invite the children to feel the weight of the sandbags in their hands. Let each child have a turn to hold, for example, three bags in one hand, and one bag in the other. Ask which hand is holding more sand, and which hand has less. Ask in which hand the sand feels heavier and in which hand the sand feels lighter.

Encourage each child to have a turn at putting up to three bags in one of the weighing pans, and the appropriate number of bags in the other pan to make it heavier than the first set

When all the children have had a turn, ask each child to put the appropriate number of bags into the second pan to make it lighter than the first set of bags.

Finally, ask all the children to put the correct number of bags in the second pan to balance ('weigh the same as') the first set of bags. Give each child a copy of the photocopiable sheet to complete. From time to time, put the weighing scales in the indoor sand tray or outdoor sand-pit, together with scoops, for the children's own exploratory play.

Support

With younger children, focus only on the terms 'more' and 'less'.

Extension

With older children, arrange experiments using two large sandwich bags. Half fill one bag with sand and allow each child to feel its weight in their hands. Let each child have a turn at putting an appropriate amount of sand in another large bag to make it heavier, lighter or the same weight as the first bag. Ask each child to feel the weight of both bags in each hand before using the scales.

HOME LINKS
At the end of the session, let the children demonstrate to their parents and carers what they have been doing. Suggest that the children do similar experiments, under supervision, at home using their hands, to explore the comparative weights of bags of sand or dried beans such as butter beans, stones, shells, conkers and so on.

MOVE THAT MOON DUST!

Learning objective

To use a programmable toy to go forwards, backwards, and to the left and right. (Knowledge and understanding of the world)

What you need

A programmable toy such as a Roamer; small, plastic bottle lid, for example, from a shampoo bottle; dry sand; Blu-Tack; plastic plate; tin-foil tube; tin foil; scissors; sticky tape; card circle (approximately 5cm radius); black sugar paper; two small-world people.

Preparation

Let the children help to make a rocket by covering the tube and card circle in foil. Cut out a door at the bottom of the rocket and secure the foil with sticky tape. Cut the card circle along the radius and bend inwards to make a cone. Secure with sticky tape and attach to the top of the rocket. Cut the sugar paper into three circles (approximately 10cm radius). Cover the small-world people in foil to make astronauts.

What to do

Explain that when astronauts visit the moon they find 'moon dust' and 'moon rocks', and use remote-controlled vehicles, such as 'moon buggies', to carry what they find back to the rocket. Stand the rocket and an astronaut on the plate, secured with Blu-Tack. Stand the other astronaut and the lid of sand (moon dust) a distance away, to the left or right of the rocket, with one black paper circle (a 'moon crater') in between. Say that the second astronaut has found some moon dust and put it in a container, and is waiting for the first astronaut to program the moon buggy to reach her, so that she can put the container on the buggy and send it back to the rocket.

Invite one child to be the first astronaut, who must program the buggy to reach the second astronaut, turning the buggy to prevent it from falling in the crater. Ask another child to be the second astronaut, and place the container on top of, or inside, the buggy. Secure it with Blu-Tack, if necessary, and encourage them to send the buggy back to the rocket.

When everyone has had a turn, ask them for further ideas for things to be carried in the buggy, for example, food or a camera, and let them continue playing independently, but be on hand for support, if necessary.

Support

With younger children, do not use any moon craters.

Extension

Use up to three moon craters with older children.

CRAB BEACH

GROUP SIZE
Five children.

TIMING
15 minutes.

Learning objective
To use a range of small and large equipment. (Physical development)

What you need
A picture of a crab; outdoor sand-pit; two small, plastic chairs or boxes; curtain; six quoits; shells; small, wheeled toy, such as a lorry; string; scissors; sheet of brown A4 card; felt-tipped pens; sticky tape; castanets.

Preparation
Involve the children in turning the sand-pit into a crab beach. Make a small cave in one corner with the curtain and chairs or boxes. Arrange the quoits ('rock pools') on the sand, with circles of shells around them. Tie a length of string (approximately 30cm) to the front of the wheeled toy. Draw a crab on the card and attach it to the wheeled toy with sticky tape, so that it can be pulled along.

What to do
Ask the children to sit around the sides of the sand-pit. Show and talk about the picture of the crab, and show the children the pull-along crab. Say that each child can have a turn to pull the crab along the sand and into the cave, as it is starting to rain. Explain that they must carefully pull the crab around the rock pools. Let one child hold the end of the string, and stand in the corner of the sand-pit, opposite the cave. Play the castanets as the child pulls the crab along, around the rock pools. Allow the child to reach the cave, before you stop playing. Say, 'It's stopped raining now', and ask the child to return to the corner.

On other occasions, let the children look through books, to draw other beach creatures to stick on small, wheeled toys, to be added to their free sand-play.

HOME LINKS
Invite the children to draw crabs on small pieces of card to take home to stick on toy cars and so on, with sticky tape, for use in sand-pits at home or on indoor 'carpet beaches'.

Support
With younger children, use only three quoits.

Extension
Invite individual older children to stand in the corner, holding the crab. Ask them to say with you, 'I'm hurrying and scurrying to my left (right) and into the cave!' as they move sideways. Encourage them to say: 'I'm hurrying and scurrying to my right (left) and out of the cave', as they return to the corner.

GROUP SIZE
Four children.

TIMING
Ten minutes.

TRICKLE, TRICKLE!

Learning objective
To create patterns. (Creative development)

What you need
Dry sand; teaspoon; two sheets of A4 card; four sheets of coloured A4 sugar paper; four seed trays (36cm x 24cm); a ruler; pencil; scissors; glue; four spreaders; sticky tape; four copies of the photocopiable sheet on page 66.

Preparation
On each sheet of card, draw a circle with a radius of 10cm. Cut around the circle and cut in half. Coil the semicircle inwards to make a cone, with a narrow hole at the point. Secure with sticky tape.

What to do
Put a sheet of coloured sugar paper inside a seed tray and hold a cone horizontally above it. Put four teaspoons of dry sand into the cone and show the children how to create patterns in the tray by gently tilting the cone and allowing the sand to trickle through the hole. Put sugar paper in the rest of the seed trays and give one to each

HOME LINKS
Let the children take a cone to use at home with sand, salt or lentils.

MULTICULTURAL LINKS
Bring in pictures (such as rangoli patterns or Greek key designs), artefacts, clothes and so on from around the world, for the children to copy. Spread glue on the patterns and trickle with sand, mixed with coloured powder paint.

child. Provide each child with a cone to hold horizontally. Put four teaspoons of sand in each child's cone and let them experiment with trickling the sand.

Roll up each child's sugar paper into a cylinder and pour the sand back into your sand container. Give each child a copy of the photocopiable sheet to put in their seed tray. Refill their cones and ask them to try to trickle their sand slowly and gently on top of the shapes. When they are proficient, ask them to spread glue over the shapes and to trickle sand on top.

At other times, leave the seed trays with sugar paper and cones in the sand tray for the children to create their own patterns and pictures. If they wish to preserve any, let them draw their patterns and pictures, and spread glue over them before trickling sand on top.

Support
Enlarge the photocopiable sheets to A3 size for younger children.

Extension
Let older children write two or three of their initials, spread them with glue and then trickle sand on top.

CHAPTER 3

Let the children use small-world play to help make sense of the world and to explore a range of play ideas.

Small-world

MAKE A QUEUE

Learning objective

To consider the consequences of their actions for themselves and others. (Personal, social and emotional development)

What you need

Four soft-toy animals; small slide (approximately 75cm high) or low jumping box; two toothpaste cartons; scissors; two pieces of A4 card; sticky tape; 16 play people.

Preparation

Cut the cartons in half, and cut the card into eight strips, each 4cm x 20cm. Fold four strips into 'zigzag steps'. Attach the steps to the top of the four half-cartons with sticky tape. Stick on an unfolded strip to each carton, to represent the slide.

What to do

Demonstrate how each toy animal wants a turn on the slide or jumping box, but that none of them understand about queuing. Improvise some amusing dialogue, for example, 'Me first! My turn!', and show the animals gently jostling for position, and how they end up crying. Ask the children what the animals should do instead. Emphasise how, in a queue, everyone is guaranteed to have a turn.

Give each child a miniature slide and four play people. Ask them to line up the play people in a queue, one behind the other, behind the slide. Encourage each child to manoeuvre their play people to take three or four turns each, in order, on the slide, as they recite the following rhyme with you: 'When we're waiting, We know what to do. We don't all rush – We make a queue!'.

Give each child a soft-toy animal to hold, and ask them to form a queue behind the slide or box, and to let their animal have three or four turns on the slide, while chanting the rhyme. On other occasions, where an appropriate and safe piece of equipment requires a queue, remind the children of the rhyme and challenge them to organise themselves.

Support

With younger children, limit the size of the group to three children, and use only three animals and three play people each.

Extension

Explain to older children the terms 'first', 'second', 'third', 'fourth.'

GROUP SIZE
Four children.

TIMING
Ten minutes.

BOOKS COME TO LIFE!

Learning objective

To retell narratives in the correct sequence, drawing on language patterns in stories, to clarify events. (Communication, language and literacy)

What you need

A copy of the photocopiable sheet on page 67; stapler; scissors; nursery-rhyme books; picture story-books; fairy-tale books; small-world figures; glove puppets; soft toys.

Preparation

Cut the photocopiable sheet into four pictures, and staple them together to make a book.

What to do

Use a small-world figure to tell the story in the book made from the photocopiable sheet, moving the small-world figure appropriately. Say 'One day a little boy/girl went for a walk on a windy day with his/her kite. It was so windy that soon the little boy/girl and the kite were blown up into the sky and into a tree, and the kite blew away. "Help!" cried the little boy/girl. His/her mum/dad came and put a ladder against the tree and climbed up the ladder and brought the little boy/girl down. They all went home and found the kite in the garden.'

Invite each child to choose two figures and use them to tell the rest of the group what is happening on one of the pages. Encourage each child to choose a familiar picture book and talk through some of it, to themselves, using a small-world figure. Ask each child to hold up one or two pages for everyone to see, and to talk about what is happening, involving the figure. The figure could be the child, who is a friend of the main character. The child figure can join in with all the events as they happen to the main character.

Add small-world figures, glove puppets and soft toys to the book area, for the children to use with their books. Some children enjoy reading a book to a toy.

Support

Use board books with younger children.

Extension

Encourage older children to retell their stories, making themselves the main character. Write down what they say and invite them to illustrate the story.

HOME LINKS
Let the children make paper finger puppets of themselves to use with a book instead of a small-world figure. Send home the puppets and books, explaining the technique to parents and carers.

MULTICULTURAL LINKS
Use small-world figures and paper finger puppets with home-language books, sent from home.

PARKING PERMITS

Learning objective
To count reliably up to 10 everyday objects. (Mathematical development)

What you need
A fit-together road layout mat; selection of play vehicles; sheet of sugar paper; black felt-tipped pen; car-park attendant's cap; sheet of yellow A4 paper; Blu-Tack.

Preparation
Draw four vertical lines on the sugar paper, to represent parking spaces and the entrance to the car-park. Number the spaces one to five. Cut the yellow paper into five rectangles, each 4cm x 2cm. Write 'Parking permit' on each one.

What to do
Take the children outside to see the nearest car-parking area to your building. Encourage the children to count the parking spaces, or to estimate how many cars could fit in the space safely. Ask them what drivers must do if the parking area is full. Explain that some car-parks have attendants, who sometimes give out parking permits. Show the children the pretend permits and say that you will be using them in a 'parking-permit game' indoors.

When you are back at the setting, ask the children to arrange the road layouts and mats as they wish on the floor area, and to begin manoeuvring their cars. At appropriate moments, ask two children at a time if they would like to come to a corner of the floor area with you, to play 'Parking permits'. Give the hat to one child to wear, who is then the car-park attendant. Lay the sugar-paper car park on the floor. Invite the attendant to put some cars in the spaces and to say how many spaces are free. Ask the second child to line up five vehicles, one behind the other, along the entrance. Ask the attendant to give the correct number of permits to the second child to stick on the windscreen of each car with a small amount of Blu-Tack. Encourage the attendant to vary the number of spaces occupied, and ask the second child to line up, on purpose, too many or not enough cars to fill the available spaces. Repeat with other children.

Support
Stick small pieces of paper, numbered 1 to 5, on the cars for younger children to match with the spaces.

Extension
Let older children use a large teaching clock to allow a pretend, limited time for each car to park.

PLANT ANOTHER ONE

Learning objective
Find out about their environment, and talk about those features they like and dislike. (Knowledge and understanding of the world)

What you need
A bunch of real or artificial foliage; scissors; Blu-Tack; sheet of white A5 paper; sheet of A4 card; green felt-tipped pen; four small-world people; two trays.

Preparation
Cut 16 miniature 'trees' from the bunch of foliage, and stick each one into a lump of Blu-Tack. Put the trees on a tray. Cut the card into 16 pieces, each 2cm x 4cm. Fold each card in half to make a stand, and draw a green seedling on one side. Put the seedlings in the second tray.

What to do
Take the children outside to look at trees in the grounds or immediate vicinity, taking the sheet of white paper with you. Talk about how trees look beautiful, and give us shade, and how they are homes for tree creatures. If possible, gently shake part of a branch and catch the insects on the paper. Let the children see you carefully returning them. Ask the children to close their eyes and imagine how bare everywhere would look without trees.

Back indoors, tell the children that in towns, cities and villages, people try not to cut down trees unless the trees are diseased. Say that in forests, trees can be grown and cut down for furniture, pencils or paper. Explain that every time woodcutters or lumberjacks cut down a tree, they plant a new seedling (a 'baby tree') to make sure that there are still trees in the world (conservation)

Give each child a small-world person and ask them to take up to four trees each to make a forest. Invite them to move their 'lumberjack' to cut down the trees, saying, 'Timber!'. Encourage the children to count the fallen trees and to replace them with the same number of seedlings. Keep miniature trees and seedlings close to your small-world people, so that the children can play 'Lumberjacks' independently.

Support
Use up to three trees each with younger children.

Extension
Talk about the conservation of trees in a rain forest.

GROUP SIZE
Up to five children.

TIMING
20 minutes.

KIND GULLIVER

Learning objective

To travel around, under, over and through balancing and climbing equipment. (Physical development)

What you need

A copy of *Gulliver's Travels* by Jonathan Swift (Penguin); balancing and climbing equipment; play people; sticky tape; Blu-Tack; a shoulder bag; wallpaper; scissors; felt-tipped pens; five copies of the photocopiable sheet on page 68; five dolls; two satsuma nets; building sets such as DUPLO.

Preparation

Cut a length of wallpaper the height of the setting's ceiling. Draw Gulliver on it with felt-tipped pens, and attach it to the wall with Blu-Tack. Arrange the equipment in a square, leaving a space in the middle.

What to do

Familiarise the children with the story of *Gulliver's Travels*. Ask the children to sit at the feet of the wallpaper Gulliver, so that they can feel as small as the Lilliputians. Say that there was an enormous flood in Lilliput, and that many people were trapped on roof-tops.

Sit the children side by side at the edge of the equipment and invite a child be Gulliver and wear the shoulder bag. Ask Gulliver to turn away, while you stick up to four play people (Lilliputians) visibly at different points on the equipment (the roof-tops), then encourage Gulliver to move carefully over the roof-tops, rescuing the Lilliputians and putting them in the shoulder bag.

When everyone has had a turn, ask the children to each build their own Lilliput with the building sets, on a table, balancing small-world people on the roof-tops. Give each child a doll to be Gulliver, with a piece of satsuma net looped over the doll's head. Ask each child to let their Gulliver walk through their Lilliput, rescuing Lilliputians in his net.

Provide each child with a copy of the photocopiable sheet to complete.

Support

Use one trapped Lilliputian on the equipment with younger children.

Extension

Instead of a bag, let older children wear a baseball cap, with a cottage-cheese pot on top of the peak, attached with sticky tape. Ask each Gulliver to put the rescued Lilliputians in the pot, travelling very carefully over the equipment so that the Lilliputians do not fall out.

HOME LINKS
Suggest to families that, at bathtime, children put a few plastic bricks on a small tray in the bath to make a flooded Lilliput, with small-world people balanced on the roof-tops. Each child could pour 'rain' from a child's watering can and then be Gulliver and rescue the Lilliputians.

GROUP SIZE
Four children.

TIMING
15 minutes.

MY PUPPET THEATRE

Learning objective
To use their imagination in art and design. (Creative development)

What you need
Four large cereal boxes, each 31cm x 19cm; two pieces of A4 card; scissors; sticky tape; felt-tipped pens; gummed shapes; sequins; glue; four glue spreaders; doilies; four copies of the photocopiable sheet on page 69.

Preparation
At the front of each box, cut out a rectangle 29cm x 8cm. At the back of each box, cut out a rectangle 28cm x 16cm. Secure the open end of each box with sticky tape. Fold and cut the pieces of card in half, lengthways.

What to do
Give each child a piece of card and ask them to decorate it with felt-tipped pens, gummed shapes and sequins. Help each child to stick their card on the front of each 'theatre'. Help each child to cut the doilies into strips and to stick them around three sides of their decorated cards, using glue, and along the top edge of their theatres with sticky tape. Encourage each child to colour in the puppets on the photocopiable sheet, cut them out, roll them into a cylinder, and secure with sticky tape, to make finger puppets.

Ask each child to choose two puppets, name them and put one on one finger of one hand, and one on one finger of the other hand. Invite each child in turn to put their theatre on the table and to sit behind it and hold up their finger puppets. Conduct a three-way conversation between yourself and the two puppets.

Support
With younger children, hold a conversation with each child holding up one puppet.

Extension
Ask older children to hold up one puppet in the theatre. Wear a puppet on one of your fingers, and conduct a conversation between yourself in 'role' and the child's puppet. Some children may like to tell a simple story using their puppets.

HOME LINKS
Let the children take home their theatres and puppets. Ask parents and carers to spare a few moments to demonstrate to the children in the setting a puppet show devised with their child.

MULTICULTURAL LINKS
Ask the children to draw, colour and cut out their own ideas for finger puppets for multicultural puppet shows, such as the Anansi stories, Jewish Purim puppets and the Divali story of Rama and Sita.

CHAPTER 4

Construction

Use a range of commercial and improvised building equipment for the children to develop skills in all Areas of Learning.

GROUP SIZE
Four children.

TIMING
Ten to 15 minutes.

HOME LINKS
Tell parents and carers that the children have been learning to set up domino rallies. Suggest that they might try this at home, using either dominoes on a table covered with a cloth or sheet to prevent scratches, or on the floor, using empty video-cassette boxes, stood vertically.

MULTICULTURAL LINKS
Arrange for the children to work in pairs on multicultural construction activities, for example, making a Chinese Dragon Boat, a Jewish harvest sukkah, Holi tissue paper garlands and Christmas paper chains.

DOMINO RALLY

Learning objective
To think about how their words and behaviour can make themselves and others feel. (Personal, social and emotional development)

What you need
Four sets of dominoes; copy of the photocopiable sheet on page 57.

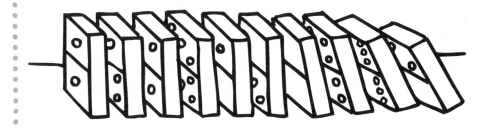

What to do
Tell the story on the photocopiable sheet. Talk about the consequences of Sarah's words. Ask what she could have said instead to Jahan so that his feelings were not hurt. Ask two children to pretend to be Sarah and Jahan and to act out a new scenario with Sarah using kind words.

Sit the children in pairs, side by side, and give each child a set of dominoes. Ask each pair of children to take turns to stand up the dominoes vertically, one behind the other, in a straight row. When each pair has used up all their dominoes, ask the children to tap the front domino together very gently, so that it causes all the other dominoes to collapse.

On other occasions, set up a special 'pairs table', with a sign and two chairs with matching cushions, or a 'pairs corner' on the floor, where two children at a time can work together on combined projects such as domino rallies, constructions, jigsaws and so on.

Support
Let younger children use half a set of dominoes each. Invite each child to stand up their dominoes horizontally, touching each other, in a zigzag shape. When each child has used up their dominoes, let them knock them down and start again.

Extension
Encourage pairs of older children to try to arrange their rallies in a curving line and also to create different levels by standing some dominoes on top of video-cassette boxes, so that they fall down on top of other dominos, similar to a waterfall.

BUILD A BARBECUE

Learning objective

To practise reading familiar and common words on an instructions sheet. (Communication, language and literacy)

What you need

One A3 copy and four A4 copies of the photocopiable sheet on page 70; two sheets of A4 card; scissors; felt-tipped pens; red, green and brown play dough; four DUPLO bases (any size); DUPLO bricks; wire cake-cooling rack; baking tray; barbecue utensils (such as a spatula, tongs and fork).

Preparation

Cut the card into four rectangles, each 15cm x 8cm. Make a few of each of the following barbecue food items from play dough: tomato slices, peppers, sausages and burgers.

What to do

Show the children the rack on the tray. Say that these are similar to a barbecue rack and tray. Talk about the utensils and put the play-dough food on to the rack. Discuss with the children any barbecues that they have experienced, and mention vegetarian sausages and veggie burgers. Explain that some grown-ups build barbecues with bricks, and that sometimes they buy a special barbecue set in a big box that contains a rack, a tray, utensils and instructions for building the walls with bricks.

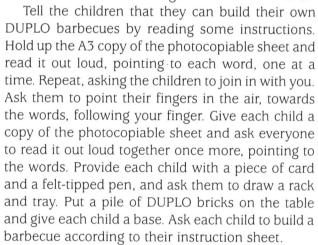

Tell the children that they can build their own DUPLO barbecues by reading some instructions. Hold up the A3 copy of the photocopiable sheet and read it out loud, pointing to each word, one at a time. Repeat, asking the children to join in with you. Ask them to point their fingers in the air, towards the words, following your finger. Give each child a copy of the photocopiable sheet and ask everyone to read it out loud together once more, pointing to the words. Provide each child with a piece of card and a felt-tipped pen, and ask them to draw a rack and tray. Put a pile of DUPLO bricks on the table and give each child a base. Ask each child to build a barbecue according to their instruction sheet.

When the children have finished, invite them to place their racks and trays on top, and to make play-dough barbecue food. At other times, leave out further, very simple instructions cards with the DUPLO, for the children to use to create a swimming pool, a double garage, stables and so on.

Support

Give younger children just the diagram to follow, and not a copy of the photocopiable sheet.

Extension

Ask older children to dictate the photocopiable sheet to adults to write the instructions on cards for other children to follow. Help the 'designers' to draw diagrams underneath the instructions.

BUNGALOW PLANS

Learning objective
To use language such as 'square', 'rectangle', 'side', 'corner', 'wide', 'long' and 'short'. (Mathematical development)

What you need
Four toy builders' hard hats; four clipboards; four sheets of A4 paper; four pencils; floor bricks; doll's-house furniture; small-world people.

Preparation
Draw a very simple outline shape of a bungalow plan on to each sheet of paper.

What to do
If possible, invite a parent who is a builder or a surveyor to the setting. Ask them to talk about their work and to show their rulers and measures, and any site plans. Alternatively, encourage staff and parents to send in any plans for home extensions. Explain to the children that a plan is a special drawing of the shape of a building.

Tell the children that they are going to be builders and give them each a hard hat and a clipboard with a building plan for a bungalow. Make sure that the children know what a bungalow is. Ask each child to take their clipboard to the 'building site', and to follow their plan to build the outside walls of their bungalow using floor bricks. Talk each child through their plan, including the words 'long', 'short', 'sides' and 'corners'. When each child has completed the outside walls, let them add inside walls with more floor bricks, before adding furniture and small-world people.

On other occasions, when the children are building, provide clipboards, paper and pencils to enable them to draw a plan beforehand.

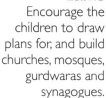

Support
Let younger children lay DUPLO bricks on top of their outline plan before using floor bricks.

Extension
Encourage older children to draw their own plans for the bungalow. Help them to measure each outside wall and to write down the length in centimetres on their plans, as well as the names of the rooms. Save the plans and return them to the children on another occasion, for example, the following day. Ask the children to follow their plans to rebuild their bungalow.

CARRY THAT PET

Learning objective
To build and construct with a wide range of objects, selecting appropriate resources, and adapting their work where necessary. (Knowledge and understanding of the world)

What you need
A real or toy pet carrier; selection of small, soft-toy pets brought from home; junk cartons (such as tall, presentation toffee cartons, cleaning-cloth cartons, shoeboxes and so on); sheets of A4 card; selection of items for joining, for example, sticky tape, glue, split-pin fasteners, ribbon, string, paper clips, treasury tags; plastic satsuma nets; scissors; straws; four trays.

What to do
Show the pet carrier to the children and explain that it was made in a factory or workshop. Talk about its features such as the lattice door and so on. Ask each child to think about how they could make one in the setting's 'workshop'. Discuss possible resources and processes. Invite some children to try to assemble all or most of the items that they think they will need on their tray. Encourage them to show the tray of items to you and tell you how they will use them before they begin working. Help other children to think through the process, one step at a time, bringing their items on their tray to show you. Be on hand as the 'workshop supervisor'.

When the pet carriers are ready, let the children 'sell' them in a 'pet shop' and also use them to carry 'sick pets' to a 'vet's surgery'. At other times, when the children are designing and making items, keep a tray for each child by the junk resources so that the children can assemble items and talk about their plan beforehand.

Support
Provide younger children with a ready-prepared lattice door, and ask them to think of ways of attaching it to the carrier and closing it.

Extension
Challenge older children to work in pairs to make carriers for snakes, insects and birds.

LIFT AND SHIFT!

Learning objective

To show awareness of space, of themselves and others. (Physical development)

What you need

A copy of *The Highway Code* (Department of Transport); eight large, transparent, plastic sandwich bags; string; scissors; newspapers; sheet of white A3 paper; black and red felt-tipped pens.

Preparation

Fill the sandwich bags with crumpled newspaper and tie the end with string to make 'mountain rocks'. Draw *The Highway Code* warning sign for falling or fallen rocks on to the white paper.

What to do

Talk about the rock-fall sign. Explain that if rocks fall on to a mountain road, sometimes bulldozers cannot drive up the narrow roads and that people have to move the rocks themselves to the roadside, standing in a human chain. Say that this is quicker and safer than if everyone walked back and forward between the rock pile and the roadside.

Ask the children to spread out in a line. Put the 'rock pile' at one end of the line. Say that the rocks are very heavy and that everyone must watch each other carefully as they give and receive the rocks slowly. Ask the first and last child to bend their knees so as not to hurt their back, as they lift and put down the rocks.

On other occasions, such as at tidy-up time, ask the children to stand in a circle, holding hands, around any areas with piles of individual items that need putting away, for example, a table top, floor space or an outside sand-pit. Pretend that the items are rocks and that the children are big bulldozers. Ask everyone to swing their arms up and down as you sing the following song to the tune of 'Here We Go Round the Mulberry Bush' (Traditional):

'Big bulldozers swing up and down,
Up and down, up and down.
Big bulldozers swing up and down,
Then they... *(pause as the children drop their hands and make them into scoops)*
Scoop up rocks like this – scoop, scoop, scoop!' *(sing the last line quickly as the children scoop up the items and put them in containers)*

Support

Let younger children sit or stand in a circle to pass the rocks.

Extension

Ask older children to stand further apart in their human chain, so that they have to stretch when moving the rocks, or ask two children to stand on low stools to enable the chain to practise reaching up and down.

SECRET TREE HOUSE

Learning objective
To explore colour and texture in three dimensions. (Creative development)

What you need
Two small food cartons, each approximately 10cm high; sticky tape; string; glue; glue spreaders; two sheets of green A4 card; sheet of white A3 paper; scissors; black felt-tipped pen; small tree or bush branch, approximately 50cm tall, with non-poisonous leaves; loose leaves or green tissue-paper leaves; bucket; old curtains; brown, black and white paints; mixing palette; paintbrushes; coffee-jar lid; three small cheese cubes; small-world people; toy animals.

Preparation
Make a small tree house from one of the food cartons, using one sheet of the green card for a roof. Glue real or tissue paper leaves on to the roof. Mix the paints to a suitable tree-bark shade, adding glue for texture. Cut out a window and a door and paint the walls. Before the children arrive, tie the house on a branch of a tree or bush at adult height.

What to do
Tell the children that during the night 'magic-tree people' have built a tree house! Talk about its camouflage. Let the children feel the texture of the tree trunk or bush stem. Just before they go home, let them see you put the cheese cubes on the lid inside the house for the tree people. Remove the cheese before the children arrive the next morning!

Stick a branch into a bucket and secure with old curtains. Let the children stick on green tissue-paper leaves with sticky tape. Ask the children to work together to make a secret tree house, similar to yours. Remind them to camouflage the roof with leaves, mix a tree-bark shade of brown paint and add glue to create a bark texture. Let the children draw a long rope ladder on the white paper in black felt-tipped pen and cut it out. Help them to tie the house on to the tree, adding the rope ladder with sticky tape. Invite the children to make up scenarios with small-world people and toy animals climbing the ladder to visit the 'magic-tree people'.

Support
Let younger children stick leaves on to the roof of a plastic doll's house with sticky tape. Invite them to paint white paper with bark-coloured paint and cover the walls.

Extension
Encourage older children to make a winter tree house by wrapping a twig in silver foil, sticking it in Blu-Tack and adding a small card cut-out glittery house.

CHAPTER 5

Outdoor play and Natural discovery

Let the children explore the outdoor area and experience different weather, changing your planned activity, if necessary, to suit the conditions.

GROUP SIZE
Up to ten children.

TIMING
Ten minutes.

HOME LINKS
Print 'Festival sheets', outlining key features, simple home activities and a photograph of the children celebrating outside (or inside). Sell the sheets inexpensively for charity.

OUR SPECIAL PLACE

Learning objective
To become familiar with, and develop a respect for, their own and others' cultures and beliefs. (Personal, social and emotional development)

What you need
A camera; sugar paper; long-armed stapler; glue; felt-tipped pens; items, props and role-play clothes relating to festivals throughout the year that are suitable for outdoor use.

Preparation
Make a large book with the sugar paper entitled 'Our special place'. Allow a double page for each festival celebrated in a year at your setting. Ask the children to decorate the cover.

What to do
After the children have experienced making cards and artefacts, listening to stories, and taking part in role-play and games associated with a particular festival, take groups outside to sit in a special place, with obvious features indicating the season, for example, under a tree or by a flower bed. Talk about the signs of the season (blossoms, scents, leaves, flowers, insects and so on). Say: 'We can tell it is now ...time, and we have been celebrating the festival of ..., which happens every year at ...time.' Sing the following to the tune of 'Tommy Thumb, Tommy Thumb' (Traditional):

> What's the season? *(x2)*
> The season of the year? *(x2)*
> It is ...time, *(name of season) (x2)*
> And ...'s here, *(name of festival) (x2)*

Remind the children about the festival activities they have been involved in indoors. Ask them for their own ideas about celebrating festivals outside, for example, Easter farmyard games involving 'farmers' and lost (replica) eggs, home-made pull-along Chinese Dragon boat races, acting out part of the Divali story, drawing chalk rangoli patterns and devising a giant version of the Hanukkah dreidel game. Let the children be as self-directing as possible and be on hand to assist. Take photographs of the activities indicating the season, and stick them in your book, with captions.

Support
Help younger children to think about celebrating outside by showing them a completed 'Our special place' book from a previous year.

Extension
Use a calendar with older children to develop a sense of when each festival takes place, then complete a copy of the photocopiable sheet on page 71.

GARDEN I SPY

Learning objective

To link sounds to letters, sounding the letters of the alphabet. (Communication, language and literacy)

What you need

String; scissors; four objects beginning with the same sound and one odd object; alphabet books; plastic or wooden alphabet letters; copy of the photocopiable sheet on page 72 for each child.

Preparation

Position or hang up one of the three objects in your outdoor area, so that it will cause maximum interest, amusement and discussion, for example, a ladle hanging from a tree branch. (If the item is likely to be damaged by bad weather, display it in a particular window that the children will see as they enter.)

What to do

As everyone arrives through the door, ask questions such as: 'Did you see something hiding in the garden?', 'What was it?', 'What sound does it begin with?' Point to the remaining three objects (two beginning with the same sound) and ask each child to name the matching pair. Hold up the alphabet book at the page displaying the corresponding letter and say: 'These things begin with..., too.'

Show each child three different letters and ask them to point to the one matching the letter in the book. Later in the day, let groups of four children make telescopes, using the photocopiable sheets. Invite them to

take them outside and spot items of their own. Ask them to lend their telescopes to each other, and to adults, saying: 'I spy, with my little eye, something beginning with..., can you see it, too?'.

Support

Give individual younger children a piece of paper with a drawing of the object in the garden and its initial letter. Ask them to stand next to the object and match the paper with it.

Extension

For older children, sometimes display or hang in the garden another item that ends with a particular sound, or has a certain sound in the middle, for example, mop.

GROUP SIZE
Three children.

TIMING
Five minutes.

MOTORBIKE COURIERS

Learning objective
To begin to relate addition to combining two sets of items. (Mathematical development)

What you need
Six small, food packets; brown wrapping paper; scissors; sticky tape; six small, plastic bottles; small basket; string; tricycle; crash helmet; two small, plastic tables and chairs; play clock; copies of the photocopiable sheet on page 73; small clipboard; pencil.

Preparation
Involve the children in wrapping the packets in the brown paper to make parcels. Tie the basket to the tricycle. Cut the photocopied sheets in half.

What to do
If possible, invite a motorbike courier to the setting to talk about their job and to show their motorbike. Explain that motorbike couriers deliver urgent things that must arrive very quickly. Say that the children can play 'Motorbike couriers' outside. Decide what is going to be delivered, and where, for example, special bandages for injured pets at a vet's surgery, or bottles of medicine for elderly people. Put a table and chair outside (the 'courier's office'). Position the other table and chair and play clock some distance away (the 'destination').

Let one child be the courier and wear the helmet, and sit on the tricycle (motorbike). Invite a second child to be the office manager and to sit in the office. Ask the third child to sit at the destination to receive the parcels. Invite the courier to ride to the office to see whether any parcels need

delivering. Invite the manager to say what the parcels contain and to give the address. Encourage the courier to put the parcels and the clipboard with the delivery sheet in the basket and to ride to the destination. Let the courier deliver the parcels, complete the sheet and return to the office to receive details of one more 'job'. When the courier has completed the second job and filled in the total box on the sheet, ask them to return to the office and 'talk through' their sheet, telling the manager how many parcels they delivered on the first and second jobs, and how many there were altogether.

At other times, provide a few props, to encourage the children to make up scenarios. For example, a baby's bottle to be delivered to a baby lamb that has just born at a farm, or a crown for a queen who's on a visit and has forgotten it.

Support
Photocopy a simplified version of the delivery sheet for younger children.

Extension
With older children, sometimes stick two delivery sheets side by side with sticky tape so that the courier needs to make three or four deliveries.

HOME LINKS
Send home a delivery sheet for the children to use at home.

GROUP SIZE
Up to four children.

TIMING
Ten minutes.

ALMOST SNAP!

Learning objective

To talk about similarities and differences between real items and drawings. (Knowledge and understanding of the world)

What you need

For each child: a copy of the photocopiable sheet on page 74, scissors, envelope, pencil, clipboard and plain paper; for general use: fine, black felt-tipped pen and ruler, if necessary (see 'Preparation'); tray; packet of 'Snap' cards.

Preparation

If any of the items on the photocopiable sheet are unlikely to be in your setting's grounds, for example, because of the season, draw an alternative in a box, cut it out and stick it on top of the existing illustration before photocopying.

What to do

Let the children watch as you draw a picture of an item in the garden, using a clipboard. Say that drawings are similar to the real item, but never identical or exactly the same. Show the children some pairs of 'Snap!' cards. Say that these are exactly the same. Let the children talk about the differences between your drawing and the real item. Hold them next to one another and say, 'Almost Snap!'

Back inside, ask each child to cut out the pictures on their photocopiable sheet, put them in an envelope and write their name on the front. Put the envelopes in a tray and go outside. Invite each child to close their eyes, take a drawing from their envelope, and go to find a similar item. Ask them to take you to it, put the drawing next to it, and say, 'Almost Snap!' Discuss with the children the similarities and differences between the two such as, size, colour, position and so on. When everyone has participated, remove the used drawings.

Keep the remaining drawings in the envelope for the children to use subsequently. At other times, have clipboards, paper and pencils readily available for the children and adults to draw items for each other to play 'Almost Snap!'.

Support

With younger children use photographs that you have taken of features in your grounds instead of drawings. Call the game 'Snap!'.

Extension

Give each child a strip of plain paper (an A4 sheet provides four strips), divided into three sections. Give everyone two different leaves and ask them to draw one of the leaves twice and the remaining leaf once. Let the children exchange strips to spot the odd one out.

HOME LINKS
Send home copies of the photocopiable sheet for children to play 'Almost Snap!'.

GROUP SIZE
Four children.

TIMING
Ten minutes.

PARENTS AND BABIES

Learning objective
To move imaginatively and confidently over obstacles. (Physical development)

What you need
Climbing equipment, for example, benches, climbing frame, tunnels and boxes; soft toys such as monkeys, kangaroos or koala bears, or pictures of these animals; scarves; sticky tape; four copies of the photocopiable sheet on page 75.

Preparation
Arrange the climbing equipment to represent a forest, with logs and fallen trees, or a jungle.

What to do
Talk to the children about how animals move and let them practise, in a clear space, being kangaroos jumping, monkeys leaping and so on. Explain that when animals are not moving on flat ground, they take care not to fall from their logs or trees. Invite the children to move along the obstacles, still pretending to be animals. Say that when animals are carrying their babies, they take even greater care and move more slowly than when they are on their own. Talk about the names of the baby animals and how they are carried. For example, kangaroo joeys are carried in their mothers' pouches, kittens are gently carried by the scruff of their necks in their mothers' teeth, and baby monkeys and koalas cling on to their mothers' backs.

Invite each child to choose a soft toy, or picture, and attach their 'baby' using a scarf or sticky tape. (Tie a joey around a child's tummy with a broadly folded scarf, or attach a drawing with sticky tape. Tie a soft-toy koala or monkey on to a child's back, using a narrowly folded scarf.) Ask the children to move carefully across the obstacles, carrying their babies.

Encourage each child to complete a copy of the photocopiable sheet.

Support
Cut the legs off a pair of used, clean tights. Tie the legs together, end-to-end. Show the children a picture of a baby elephant (calf), walking behind its mother, holding on to her tail with its trunk. Ask one child to be the mother elephant and tie the tights around their waist, leaving a tail. Ask another child to be a calf and to hold on to the mother's tail, using their arm as a trunk. Ask the mother elephant to lead the calf.

Extension
Let older children make a large illustrated book about how animals carry their babies.

HOME LINKS
Ask the children to bring soft toy baby animals from home. Let the children use animal reference books and encyclopaedias at the setting to find out how the babies are carried.

GROUP SIZE
Up to ten children.

TIMING
Ten minutes.

HEDGEHOGS HIBERNATE!

Learning objective

To match movements to music. (Creative development)

What you need

A copy of the photocopiable sheet on page 59; one old sheet or table-cloth, preferably in a plain dark colour; autumn leaves; climbing frame; battery-operated tape recorder; tape; percussion instruments such as tambourines, maracas, xylophone, castanets and triangles; hedgehog dirt-scraper shoe brush (if possible) or a scrubbing brush.

Preparation

Place the sheet or table-cloth on top of the climbing frame and cover with leaves.

What to do

Before going outside, talk to the children about how, in autumn, some animals, such as hedgehogs, start to hibernate. Let them feel the hedgehog-like, spiky shoe brush or scrubbing brush.

Teach the children the song on the photocopiable sheet and make a recording of the children singing, to the accompaniment of percussion instruments, for example, tambourines for the first verse, maracas for the second, a xylophone for the third, castanets for the fourth, and triangles for the fifth.

Take the children outside with the tape recorder. Stand the children around the climbing frame and ask them to pretend to be hedgehogs about to hibernate in the autumn. Play the first verse of the song, as you and another adult remove the sheet or table-cloth and gently shake it, to enable the leaves to fall to the ground. Continue playing the tape as the children make movements to the music.

On other occasions, put the tape recorder on a table outside for the children to operate and make up their own dances.

Support

Before taking young children outside, let them practise 'shuffling', 'curling up', 'nibbling' and 'stretching'.

Extension

Invite older children to suggest ideas about other animals that hibernate, for example, bears and snakes. Adapt the words of the song on the photocopiable sheet accordingly, record the children singing and let them pretend to be these animals.

HOME LINKS
Fold a piece of brown sugar paper, approximately 40cm x 30cm, in half. Ask the children to write 'The hedgehog song' at the top, and to paint or draw some hedgehogs. Place a copy of the song sheet inside and let the children take them home.

CHAPTER 6

By providing a water tray and a range of equipment, you can offer opportunities for explorative play.

Water

GROUP SIZE
Up to six children.

TIMING
15 minutes.

ALL CLEAN!

Learning objective
To manage aspects of personal hygiene. (Personal, social and emotional development)

What you need
A copy of the photocopiable sheet on page 61 for each child; washing-up bowl of warm water; soap; paper towels.

Preparation
Fold the photocopied sheets along the dotted line to hide the words.

What to do
Sit the children around the table with the bowl in front of you. Show them that your hands need washing, for example, that you have some paint on them. Talk about why and when we must wash our hands. Demonstrate how you wet your hands and rub the soap to make a lather. Say why we must rinse the soap from our hands and dry them properly. Remove the bowl and teach the children the first verse of the song on the photocopiable sheet, asking them to make appropriate hand actions.

Talk about face-washing, saying that some people do not use soap, because faces do not get so dirty as hands. Sing the second verse. Discuss hair-washing and how a grown-up needs to help with this. Sing the third verse. Talk about brushing teeth and how some grown-up help is also needed with this. Sing the last verse.

Give each child a copy of the photocopiable sheet, with the bottom strip not visible, and sing through the song together, with the children pointing to the words. Ask them to draw line to join the pictures to the matching words. Each time that the children wash their hands at the setting, encourage them to sing the first verse of the song.

Support
Give younger children a doll to use instead of a copy of the photocopiable sheet. Sing the song again and ask them to 'wash' the doll's hands, faces and hair and to 'dry' them with a paper towel. Give each child an inexpensive toothbrush to use while singing the last verse.

Extension
Unfold the photocopiable sheet for older children and invite them to complete the strip at the bottom of the sheet.

HOME LINKS
Invite the children to draw a picture of themselves from the waist upwards. Let them take the pictures home, together with four peel-off star stickers. Ask families to put a sticker next to their children's hands, face, hair and teeth to show that the children can wash their hands and face independently and is happy to co-operate with hair-washing and teeth-cleaning.

GROUP SIZE
Four children.

GROUP SIZE
Four children.

TIMING
15 minutes.

MESSAGE IN A BOTTLE

Learning objective
To learn to write alphabet letters. (Communication, language and literacy)

What you need
A carpeted area; large, plastic bottle; two sheets of A5 paper; pencil; blue crayon; cotton thread; scissors; four cushions; bunch of artificial leaves; lid of dry sand; shoulder bag.

Preparation
Put the leaves in a corner to represent a desert island together with the lid of sand. Draw a simple map, using the blue crayon for the sea.

What to do
Talk about 'leaky ships' in the 'olden days' and how they sometimes let in water so that sailors had to abandon ship and swim to land, possibly to a desert island. Explain how sailors might send a message in a bottle.

Invite two children to be sailors, one of them wearing the shoulder bag diagonally, with the bottle, paper and pencil inside. Put two cushions (to represent the ship) on the floor, one behind the other. Ask the sailors to 'name the ship' and to sit in it. Tell them to pretend to be swept overboard in a storm and to swim to the desert island. Encourage one child to write 'Help' on the message, and the other to draw the ship, showing its name. Help both children to sign their names. Invite them to pour a little sand into the bottle to show rescuers that they are 'on land'. Explain that the rescuers will be able to work out where they are by looking at their map.

Help the sailors to make a hole in the message with the pencil point and to attach a length of thread for easy retrieval. Ask them to push the message into the bottle, put on the cap and toss it into the sea. Using the other two cushions as the rescue ship, ask two more sailors to sit in it, find the bottle, and save the shipwrecked sailors. At other times, leave small, plastic bottles in the writing corner for the children to create their own messages.

Support
Help younger children just to sign their names on the message.

Extension
Ask older children to write or dictate sea-rescue stories.

HOME LINKS
Help the children to write the message: 'Please help to dry me', to take home and put in a small plastic bottle. Encourage them to play 'Shipwrecks' at bathtime, tossing the bottles into their bathwater sea for grown-ups to rescue.

MULTICULTURAL LINKS
Ask families to write 'Help' in various languages. Pretend that the desert island is near different countries.

GROUP SIZE
Five children.

TIMING
20 minutes.

HOW THIRSTY?

Learning objective
To use language, such as 'more' and 'less'. (Mathematical development)

What you need
Five copies of the photocopiable sheet on page 76; five pencils; four teddy bears; four transparent plastic tumblers; plastic jug; water; nine chairs; table.

Preparation
Sit each bear in a chair, side by side, behind the table. Fill the jug with water.

What to do
Invite the children to sit facing the table. Talk about how, on hot days, we can become thirsty and how water is the best drink to stop us feeling thirsty. Tell the children that some of the bears are thirsty, they are at a café, and that you are the waiter or waitress. Invite the children to choose a

name for each bear. Ask each bear how much water they would like. Pretend to be each bear replying, and pour the appropriate amount of water for them. Imagine that the first bear has just had a drink and is not thirsty, so leave the first tumbler empty, the second bear is a little thirsty so pour a little water into the second tumbler, the third bear is quite thirsty and would like half a glassful and the fourth bear is very thirsty so would like a lot of water. Compare the tumblers, talking about which bear has more, or less, water.

Let the children take turns at being customers and the waiter or waitress. At the end of the last turn, remind everyone about how much water each child had. Ask the children to complete the photocopiable sheet using their own level of emergent writing to write everyone's names. At other times, let the children play 'Cafés' at the water tray with plastic tumblers and a jug.

Support
With younger children use only three bears, one requiring an empty tumbler, one needing a little water and one a lot.

Extension
With older children, make another copy of the photocopiable sheet and draw lines on three of the tumblers to indicate a little water, half a glassful and a whole glassful. Cut out all four tumblers and give one to each of four children. Ask each one to ask the waiter or waitress for the amount of water shown on their drawing.

HOME LINKS
Give each child a blank photocopiable sheet to take home and complete with names of family members, after playing 'Cafés'.

GROUP SIZE
Four children.

TIMING
Ten minutes.

THIN ICE

Learning objective

To investigate their environment through the medium of touch. (Knowledge and understanding of the world)

What you need

Four used, shallow plastic or foil food containers; water; small-world people; four miniature plastic dogs , for example, from maths sorting sets; string; scissors.

Preparation

Cut the string into four pieces, each approximately 10cm long. Tie each 'lead' to a plastic dog. Cover the bottom of each container with water approximately 1cm deep. Put the container in the freezer and keep checking until a thin layer of ice is formed. Remove from the freezer.

What to do

Give each child a container of thin ice. Say that the container is a pond in winter. Explain that the ice may look solid, but often it is very thin. Let the children gently feel and tap the ice.

Talk about the dangers of thin ice. Tell a story about a family out walking their dog on a lead, near a frozen pond. Say that the dog ran away and on to the ice. Ask the children to say what happened next, and to think about which member of the family could grab the dog's lead and pull it out. Ask the children to select small-world people to represent the family. Give each child a dog on its lead, and encourage them to talk through their own version of the story, using the small-world people and letting their dogs fall through the ice. Ask each child to tell their story to the others. At other times, put a washing-up bowl of thin ice in the water tray, with small-world people, animals and so on and let the children make up their own scenarios.

Support

Let younger children make the appropriate actions with small-world people and dogs on leads, as they listen to you telling the story.

Extension

Ask older children about other ways of rescuing the dog. Ask what they could use for these rescues, for example, a twig for a tree branch, lollipop stick for a plank, satsuma net and so on.

HOME LINKS
Cut a transparent polythene bag into rough ovals, approximately 10cm across. Ask each child to glue one on to a piece of A4 paper to represent a frozen pond. Let each child take home the sheet to make up a story about the pond, draw the characters and bring their picture back to the setting.

SWIMMING

Learning objective

To recognise the importance of keeping healthy and those things which contribute to this. (Physical development)

What you need

A copy of the photocopiable sheet on page 60.

What to do

Explain to the children about the importance of exercise in keeping healthy and how swimming is excellent exercise. Talk about going swimming in the sea on holiday and swimming in a pool. Discuss the differences between the two and how both make our bodies feel (beating heart, tingling blood, stretched muscles and so on). Talk about how all these sensations are good for our bodies.

Ask the children to pretend that they are on a beach holiday. Let them sit on the 'beach' and listen as you recite the first poem. Invite them to stand up and make the appropriate actions, as you recite the poem again. Ask for further ideas of swimming actions to do in the sea and incorporate them into the poem.

Tell the children that they are now going to pretend to swim in a pool. Ask them to sit at the 'poolside' and to listen to the second rhyme. Repeat the rhyme, asking the children to make appropriate actions. Ask for further ideas for actions and words for the poem. At other times, designate a space as either the sea or a swimming-pool, and ask the children to 'go swimming' and to describe their actions to you.

Support

Let younger children pretend to be parents or carers. Give them a doll and encourage them to teach it to swim in the sea or in a pool.

Extension

Invite individual older children be a swimming instructor at a pool. Give them a whistle and let them conduct a lesson.

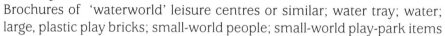

GROUP SIZE
Four children.

TIMING
20 minutes.

WATERWORLD

Learning objective
To use their imagination to design an object. (Creative development)

What you need
Brochures of 'waterworld' leisure centres or similar; water tray; water; large, plastic play bricks; small-world people; small-world play-park items (slides and so on); large, plastic animals, especially elephants and giraffes; plastic leaves; Blu-Tack; scissors; food packaging, including foil pie dishes; sticky tape; construction sets such as DUPLO, marble runs and so on; circular margarine tubs; straws; 15cm-long ruler; small, plastic watering can; plastic tray; table.

Preparation
Stick small 'trees' of leaves in lumps of Blu-Tack. Cut strips of foil from the pie dishes (approximately 15cm x 4cm). Curve the sides upwards, to create chutes, for the children to attach to animals later with sticky tape, to create animal water chutes.

What to do
Ask the children about their experiences of visiting water leisure centres. Discuss the features that they enjoy such as animal water chutes in the toddlers' areas, 'twisty-turny' water slides and tunnels, jacuzzis, spa baths and so on. Look at the pictures in the brochures together. Ask for ideas for turning the water tray into a 'waterworld'. Let the children look at the animals, construction sets and packaging for initial ideas, for example, using the margarine pots and straws for jacuzzis, and the ruler as a diving board. Help the children to arrange a few play bricks at the sides of the water tray to create different levels and areas. Put a table next to the water tray, with the tray on top. Suggest that the children build the 'changing and shower area' on the tray with the construction sets, using the watering can as a shower.

Support
Help younger children to practise making one kind of feature together, at the same time, for example, the margarine-tub jacuzzis or the animal water chutes.

Extension
Ask older children for ideas for creating the effect of a wave machine (blowing the water together, or gently tilting the water tray and so on).

HOME LINKS
Show families the waterworld model when the children are collected from the setting to inspire similar ideas in the bath or washing-up bowl at home.

EARLY YEARS ACTIVITY CHEST Structured play

CHAPTER 7

Art and craft

Encourage each child to express their individuality by giving free reign to their creativity and imagination through the medium of art and craft.

PHOTO-FRAME CARDS

Learning objective
To begin to understand different cultural and religious celebrations. (Personal, social and emotional development)

What you need
A few photograph frames; examples of greetings cards incorporating a photograph, if possible; used greetings cards, for example, for Easter, Eid and Divali; four copies of the photocopiable sheet on page 77; sheets of coloured A4 card; scissors; rulers; glue; sticky tape; felt-tipped pens.

Preparation
Cut the card into four pieces, each 17cm x 13cm.

What to do
Talk about how photographs are used as gifts, sometimes on cards, and show the children the examples. Look at the patterns on the photograph frames. Encourage the children to tell you about family cultural or religious celebrations for which a frame card could be appropriate. Help the children to write their greeting on the cut pieces of card, for example, 'Happy Grandparents' Day', 'Happy Birthday', 'Happy Divali' and so on.

Ask the children to decorate the frame on the photocopiable sheet using felt-tipped pens. If the card is to celebrate a festival, encourage them to use symbols from the greetings cards (for example, stars and a crescent moon for Eid), either cut out or copied. When the children have decorated their frame, invite them to cut it out, stick it on a piece of A4 card and trim it. Give the children a small piece of rolled-up sticky tape to attach their small greetings card in the centre. This can be replaced with a photograph of the child, possibly with siblings (but make sure that families agree to this first), and a card hinge (12cm x 4cm) can be stuck on to the back. The frame cards can be turned into conventional cards, such as for Eid, as the Islamic religion forbids making pictures of living things. Stick a piece of card down one side of the back so that it opens. Inside, let each child write, 'Love from…'.

Support
Cut out and stick the frames on to card, for younger children.

Extension
Encourage older children to make repeating patterns of two or three symbols on their frame.

GROUP SIZE
Four children.

TIMING
20 minutes.

FANTASTIC CREATURES

Learning objective

To sustain attentive listening and respond to what they have heard. (Communication, language and literacy)

What you need

A copy of the photocopiable sheet on page 58; piece of paper and pencil for each child; sufficient crayons to ensure that each child has the same range of colours.

What to do

Read the story 'My Hug-o-saurus' on the photocopiable sheet to the children. Tell them that you are going to say what a fantastic creature looks like. Ask the children to listen very carefully as you describe the creature and to draw what you say. Start to describe each part of the creature slowly, giving the children plenty of time to draw it. Pause after describing each part of the creature. Say, for example, 'Now I'll tell you about its legs'.

When the children have finished, let them compare pictures, think of names for their creatures, and make up stories about them. At other times when the children are drawing, encourage one child to be the teacher who describes a picture for the others to draw.

Support

After you have described each part of the creature, ask younger children to draw the part in the air with you at the same time. Then ask them to draw the same part on paper.

Extension

Invite older children to play 'Surprise fantastic creatures', in which the finished drawing is not revealed until the end of the game, as a surprise. Sit the children at opposite ends of a table, with a screen between them, for example, a shallow box on its side. Ask the first child to describe the creature to the second child, who draws it. After each part of the creature has been drawn, ask the second child to say, 'Ready!'. Listen to the first child's description so that when the finished drawing is revealed, and the first child is checking it, you can assess the first child's recall of their own description.

HOME LINKS
Let the children take home their pictures of the fantastic creatures. Ask families to play the game and to send the pictures back to the setting for everyone to see. Stick them in a large book. Challenge the children to use recyclable materials to make 3-D models of some of the creatures.

PATTERN IT

Learning objective

To talk about, recognise and recreate simple patterns. (Mathematical development)

What you need

A few patterned table mats; different-coloured counting cubes; white A4 paper; six transparent, plastic document sleeves; felt-tipped pens (the same colours as the cubes); scissors; sticky tape; samples of simple patterns on fabrics, clothing and crockery; six copies of the photocopiable sheet on page 78.

Preparation

Draw a border of 14 squares around the paper and make five photocopies. Colour the squares of the original copy, in a repeating pattern of two colours, and put it in a sleeve. Cut off the 'holed' band at the side of the sleeve, and secure the open end with sticky tape to make a table mat. Cut off the bands from the remaining sleeves.

What to do

Show the children the table mats and talk about the patterns. Say that it is fun to make a pattern and to copy it on to something to use, such as a table mat. Hold up the 'sleeved' paper and tell the children that they can make a similar table mat. Talk about the pattern and ask them to name the colours. Give each child a copy of the patterned paper and some cubes. Invite them to arrange the cubes in a repeating pattern of two colours and ask them to colour their squares to match the pattern. Help each child to slide their table mat into a sleeve and secure the side with sticky tape.

Talk about the patterns on the other items. Ask the children to complete the photocopiable sheet, reminding them to try making their patterns repeat with two features.

Support

With younger children, make a repeating pattern of cubes for them to match with the cubes underneath, before asking them to make their own cube pattern.

Extension

Ask older children to cut out their patterned items from the photocopiable sheet, glue them on to separate sheets of paper and incorporate them into pictures.

GROUP SIZE
Four children.

TIMING
20 minutes.

FAMILY TREE

Learning objective
To find out about past events in their own and in their families' lives. (Knowledge and understanding of the world)

What you need
A copy of a family tree or a diagram in a book; small three-branched twig for each child; kitchen foil; Blu-Tack; two sheets of coloured A4 card; scissors; hole-punch; four glue sticks; four pencils; decorative string; for each child: three small photocopied photographs: one of the child, one of a parent and one of a grandparent, preferably as babies or children.

Preparation
Prior to the activity, send a letter home asking for three small photocopied photographs of the child, a parent or carer and a grandparent. Ask families to talk about a family anecdote in relation to each photograph.

What to do
Explain to the children that sometimes families like to write down their names, and the names of everybody in their family, in the shape of a tree, called a family tree. Show an example, if possible, or a diagram in a book.

Say that it is fun to find out lots of things about everyone in a family. Give each child a three-branched twig and help them to cover it with silver foil and to stick the bottom in a lump of Blu-Tack. Invite each child to draw an oval line around each of their photocopied photographs and to cut them out. Ask each child to cut out three card ovals, each slightly larger than the photograph, and to glue the photographs on to the ovals. Encourage each child to punch a hole at the top of each oval, thread some decorative string through each one, and hang them on their tree.

When the trees are finished, ask each child to tell the rest of the group about their photographs. On other occasions, leave out some prepared silver trees, card ovals, decorative string and felt-tipped pens. Let the children make their own trees or pendants, with drawings of family members, as gifts.

Support
Cut out the photographs and the card ovals for younger children and help them to tie them on to their trees.

Extension
Ask older children to draw their trees on paper.

HOME LINKS
Ask parents, carers and grandparents to come in and tell the children more about the photographs, possibly bringing with them some traditional toys or other items.

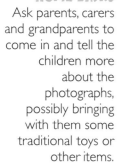

GROUP SIZE
Four children.

TIMING
15 minutes.

WALKING FINGERS

Learning objective
To develop their awareness of co-ordination and control in movement. (Physical development)

What you need
Ready-mixed or powder paint; saucers; tissues; white painting paper.

Preparation
Put a different colour of paint in each saucer.

What to do
Talk to the children about different ways of moving with our legs, for example, walking, running, jumping, hopping, sliding (on ice) and so on. Practise the movements, asking the children whether the movements are fast or slow, light or heavy, and whether one foot or two feet are used.

Ask the children to pretend that their fingers are legs and to move

them in the air, as if they were walking, running, jumping, hopping or sliding. Say that it is fun to dip fingers into paint and move them across the paper as if they were legs. Demonstrate, by dipping your forefinger and third finger in one colour of paint, and walking them across the paper. Invite the children to dip their fingers in one colour of paint and to make 'fingerprints' on the paper, as if they were footprints, for walking, running, jumping, hopping and sliding. Ask them to think about whether they will move their fingers quickly or slowly, lightly or heavily, and whether they will be using one finger or two. Let them choose a different colour to represent each kind of movement.

Practise moving like elephants, kangaroos, ants, snakes and so on, and ask the children to make these movements with their fingers, in the air, and then on to the paper, with their fingers dipped in paint. On other occasions, when the children are painting pictures with brushes, encourage them to think about using finger-painting to create special effects for parts of their pictures.

Support
Give younger children, who may be a little nervous about dipping their fingers in paint, cotton buds to use at first.

Extension
Ask older children how they could represent 'crawling' across the page, for example, dipping their knuckles in the paint, bending their fingers and moving them over the paper.

HOME LINKS
Encourage parents and carers to take their children to the park or soft-play centre to enjoy free play.

GROUP SIZE
Four children.

TIMING
15 minutes.

THIS COULD BE A...

Learning objective

To explore 2-D irregular shapes by relating them to real items. (Creative development)

What you need

Four copies of the photocopiable sheet on page 79; four pencils; four long, beaded necklaces or thick threading laces; four rectangles of tissue paper (14cm x 10cm); four sheets of white A3 paper; glue; felt-tipped pens.

What to do

Hold up a necklace and say that you are going to turn it into all kinds of different things. Put the necklace on a table and show the children how you can make different items with it, for example, a balloon, sausage, wiggly snake, heart and a house. Give each child a necklace and let them experiment with making and interpreting each others' shapes. Provide each child with a rectangle of tissue paper and ask them to tear it round the edges very carefully. Invite them to say what their torn shapes look like. Ask them to glue their shapes in the centre of the white paper and to add details with felt-tipped pens.

Give each child a copy of the photocopiable sheet to complete. At other times, leave out in the art area, sheets of white paper each with a torn piece of tissue paper glued in the centre, for the children to add further details to.

Support

Before providing younger children with the necklaces or laces, give them regular shapes, such as a circle, square, triangle and rectangle, cut from white paper. Ask the children to think about different things that the shapes could be.

Extension

Invite older children to sit in pairs and for one child to 'take their pencil for a walk', and draw an irregular shape in the centre of a piece of paper. Let the other child turn the shape into whatever they like by adding extra details to it.

HOME LINKS
Give each child a piece of A3 paper. Help them to fold their paper into sections for each family member who can draw. Ask each child to draw the same irregular shape, as far as possible, in all the sections. Encourage the children to turn the first shape into a 'special thing' by adding details. Let them take home their sheets for each family member to turn their shape into something else. Ask everyone to bring back their shapes to the setting.

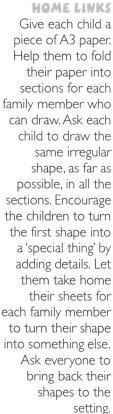

CHAPTER 8

Encourage the children to use malleable materials to create models of animals, buildings and arfetfacts.

Clay and dough

FANTASTIC SNAKE

Learning objective
To be confident to try a new activity. (Personal, social and emotional development)

What you need
An adult's plain sock; two buttons; small piece of red paper; scissors; sticky tape; toilet tissue; large bowl of play dough (any colour); enough wooden baseboards to cover a table in a diagonal line; items to stick in the play dough to create different kinds of 'snake skin', for example, shells, buttons, fir cones, milk-bottle tops; four copies of the photocopiable sheet on page 80.

Preparation
Cut out a small tongue shape from the red paper and stick it on to the toe end of the sock. Attach the buttons for eyes with sticky tape. Lay the boards end to end, diagonally, across the table.

What to do
Put the sock on your hand to make a snake's head. Say that the 'fantastic snake' needs an amazing body. Take the sock off your hand and stuff it with toilet tissue. Position it at one end of the boards. Place the play-dough bowl on the table and ask the children to take out a lump at a time to put together on the boards to make the snake. Ask the first child to suggest something to stick in the play dough to make a fantastic snake. Let the next child find the items and stick them in the play dough, where and how the first child describes. Continue until the whole snake is covered.

Give each child a copy of the photocopiable sheet and invite them to decorate their section of snake, either by drawing three kinds of patterns or using collage items, and to join their section with their friends', then make a snake's head. Sometimes, when the children are working with play dough, encourage them to put two or more boards, side by side, and collaborate on a very long item, that could then be drawn.

Support
Let younger children work together to decorate the snake by suggesting items to make imprints in the play dough such as cones, Sticklebricks, DUPLO and so on.

Extension
Show older children pictures of snakes and talk about the patterns. Ask them for ideas on reproducing the patterns in the fantastic snake.

GROUP SIZE
Four children.

TIMING
Three ten-minute sessions and one 15-minute session (the last ten-minute session may be omitted).

PET ROCKS

Learning objective
To explore the meaning of new words. (Communication, language and literacy)

What you need
Four lumps of air-drying clay, each the size of a medium potato; four wooden baseboards covered in hessian or textured material; water-based paints; medium paintbrushes; PVA glue, four glue pots, sticks and water (optional); four plastic mirrors; sheet of white A4 card; scissors; four pencils; four erasers; felt-tipped pens; Blu-Tack.

Preparation
If the children are varnishing their 'pet rocks', fill each glue pot with a solution of two parts PVA glue to one part water before the third session. Before the last session, cut the card into four ovals, each 4cm wide.

What to do
Say that the children can make a clay 'pet rock' which will have an 'expression' to show its feelings. Make some obvious facial expressions yourself, for example, happy and sad. Ask everyone to join in, guessing each other's expressions, and talking about when they experience these feelings. Give each child a lump of clay on a board and ask them to make a smooth pet rock. Leave them to air-dry. When dried, ask everyone to paint their rocks and, again, leave them to dry. At the next session, if desired, the rocks can be varnished with the PVA mixture.

At the last session, talk about 'emotions' words that the children might not be used to, for example, 'surprised', 'furious', 'amused' and 'exhausted'. Give each child their painted rock and ask them to choose to make one of the following: 'Surprised Sophie (or Sam)', 'Furious Freddy (or Flora)', 'Amused Andrew (or Alina)', 'Exhausted Ella (or Edward)'. Let the children look in a mirror to practise making their expression, noticing especially their eyebrows, eyes and mouth. Encourage each child to draw their expression on an oval card with a pencil, using an eraser if necessary, before using felt-tipped pens. Ask each child to attach their oval face to their rock with Blu-Tack. Provide ready-drawn faces whenever the children are using clay, on subsequent occasions, in case they wish to use them.

Support
With younger children, use familiar vocabulary, for example, 'happy', 'sad', 'cross', 'tired'.

Extension
Let older children try to make expressions in the clay using their fingers or implements.

HOME LINKS
Let each child take home their pet rock with a blank, face card. Ask families to help their children to draw another pet-rock character which could replace the initial card.

Four children.

Ten minutes.

DINOSAUR EGGS

Learning objective

To begin to use the vocabulary involved in subtracting. (Mathematical development)

What you need

Four lumps of play dough of any colour (adult's fist-sized); four model dinosaurs; 16 miniature dinosaurs such as from maths sorting sets, or use drawings on very small pieces of card; sheet of grey A4 card; black felt-tipped pen; scissors.

Preparation

Fold the A4 card into quarters. Draw a rough circle shape in each and cut them out.

What to do

Say that mother dinosaurs laid eggs, often in hollows in the ground. Give each child four miniature or card dinosaurs and a lump of play dough. Invite the children to break their play dough into four and to make four circle shapes. Ask them to put a 'baby dinosaur' inside each circle and to roll the play dough around it gently to form an egg. When the eggs are made, give each child a card 'hollow' and let them put their eggs inside. Give each child a 'mother dinosaur' to keep watch. Ask each child to say how many eggs are in their hollow.

Then, say that the first egg is ready to hatch. Encourage each child to make their mother dinosaur gently nudge one egg out of the hollow with her mouth, for the egg to hatch properly.

When the hatching eggs have been removed, ask the children to say how many eggs are left. Let each child make their first egg appear to hatch, by revealing the baby dinosaur inside.

Say to the children that there are three eggs left in each hollow. Ask them to make the mother dinosaur nudge out two more, which are ready to hatch at the same time. Ask how many eggs are left. Continue the activity, verbalising what happens when the last egg hatches. When the children are playing independently with play dough, provide mother dinosaurs for them to make up their own egg-hatching scenarios involving subtraction.

Support

With younger children, play the game with only one egg being nudged at a time.

Extension

Ask an older child to close their eyes while another hides some of their eggs. The first child must work out how many are hidden.

Let the children take home card baby dinosaurs inside play-dough eggs to play the game at home.

Play an Easter farm game using stand-up card 'mother hens' and card 'baby chicks' inside the play-dough eggs.

GROUP SIZE
Four children.

TIMING
20 minutes.

CLAY TOWN

Learning objective
To find out about their environment and to learn some features of buildings. (Knowledge and understanding of the world)

What you need
Four clipboards; four sheets of white A4 paper; four pencils; four lumps of ready-coloured air-drying clay (adult's fist-sized); four wooden baseboards covered in hessian or textured material; four plastic knives; modelling tools; road layout; small-world people.

What to do
Take the children on a walk to look at some local buildings, or alternatively take photographs of some buildings that the children are likely to pass on their journey to the setting. Ask them to choose one building and to draw it on their clipboards. Let them focus on the most obvious features such as windows, doors and roofs.

Back inside, give each child a lump of clay on a board and help them to 'cut and slice' their clay into cuboid or cube shapes with the plastic knife, Encourage them to use a cuboid or cube shape for the main part of their building. Ask them to look at their drawing to remind them about the number and position of windows and doors. Let them use the modelling tools to score these in the clay. Help them to make simple triangular prism shapes for sloping roofs by cutting and slicing a shallow cuboid shape, gently pressing each end into a

triangular point, then smoothing the middle section of their roof between their hands. Let each child use the tools to score the patterns of roof tiles. Help them to lift their roof and place it on top of their building.

When the buildings are finished, ask the children to set out the road layout and arrange the buildings, small-world people and vehicles. At other times, when the children are working independently with clay, provide some ready-cut cuboid, cube and triangular prism shapes to inspire 'building work'.

HOME LINKS
Ask families to help their children to make a simple drawing of their home to bring to the setting for them to make clay models.

MULTICULTURAL LINKS
Let children make models of places of worship such as a church, mosque or synagogue.

Support
Draw very simple house outlines for younger children to lay rolled 'spaghetti strings' of clay on top.

Extension
Provide older children with pictures of different kinds of buildings, to inspire their modelling such as a cottage, skyscraper and an igloo.

HOT HANDS

Learning objective
To recognise some of the changes that happen to the body, during exercise and activity. (Physical development)

What you need
A pair of rubber gloves; two large carrots; two lumps of Blu-Tack; six lumps of clay (adult's fist-sized); six wooden baseboards covered in hessian or textured material; sheet of A4 paper; pen.

Preparation
Stick each carrot upright into a lump of Blu-Tack. Place a rubber glove over each carrot.

What to do
Show the pair of rubber gloves to the children and say they are a 'pair of hands'. Explain that when hands manipulate clay, they begin to feel different. Give each child a lump of clay and encourage them to play freely, letting them verbalise what their hands are doing. Jot down the words that they use.

After five minutes ask how their hands are feeling and whether they are beginning to feel hot. Encourage them to say which hand movements make their hands feel hot and which do not, for example, patting, stroking and poking (not hot), squeezing, pinching and twisting (hot).

Invite everyone to sing the following song to the tune of 'Here We Go Round the Mulberry Bush' (Traditional) and to make the appropriate actions with their clay:

'This is the way we pat the clay, *(repeat twice)*
And our hands don't feel hot!
This is the way we squeeze the clay, *(repeat twice)*
And our hands feel hot!'

Whenever the children are using clay, ask them to talk about how their hands feel.

Support
To help younger children learn the words to describe how they manipulate clay, watch them as they explore the clay freely. Invite a child to demonstrate one of their actions, such as poking. Ask everyone to repeat the same action together as you all sing, 'We all poke the clay', to the tune of 'The Farmer's in His Dell'.

Extension
Let older children experiment with rolling clay with their hands. Ask them whether their hands start to feel hot, or not, when they are rolling the clay slowly. What happens when they roll the clay quickly? Do their hands feel hot if they use a rolling-pin?

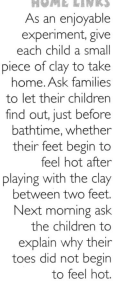

CLAY GIFT SHOP

Learning objective

To express their decorative and pattern-making ideas. (Creative development)

What you need

A pen holder (any design); candle-holder (any design); four lumps of ready-coloured air-drying clay (adult's fist-sized); four wooden baseboards covered in hessian or textured material; four rolling-pins; pastry cutters; four plastic knives; four candles; modelling tools; four old ballpoint pens; items for making imprints such as old Sticklebricks and DUPLO, potato masher, meat tenderiser, pastry wheel and keys.

What to do

Show the pen holder and candleholder to the children and explain that people give them as gifts. Say that the children can make one of them from clay and can sell them in a 'clay gift shop' to the person collecting them at the end of the session. Explain that the money will go to charity.

For the pen holder, give each child a baseboard and a lump of clay. Ask them to roll it out and cut a strip of clay, approximately 3cm x 14cm, with a plastic knife. Give each child a used ballpoint pen to make four holes at intervals of two centimetres. Ask each child to choose tools and items to score designs or make imprints in the spaces between the holes.

For the candle-holder, ask each child to roll out their clay to a thickness of approximately two centimetres. Give them a pastry cutter or a plastic knife, to cut out the shape of the holder, and a candle to make a hole in the centre. Let them decorate the holder by scoring designs or making imprints. When the gifts are completely dry, let each child sell their own at the shop. Explain that only an adult may light candles.

Support

Let younger children make pebble-shaped paperweights from the clay.

Extension

Encourage older children to make clay pendants.

Domino friends

Sarah was four years old. Her best friend was a boy called Jahan, who was also four. They lived next door to one another and were in the same nursery class at Olive Road Primary School. Usually, they played very well together, but sometimes they would SQUABBLE! If they were doing a floor jigsaw together, they would sometimes want the same piece. Then they would argue and that would upset them both. The grown-ups in their families, or their teacher, Mrs Taylor, would help them to chat about it and to say 'sorry' to one another. Sarah and Jahan would then carry on doing the jigsaw together as happily as could be!

One day, Sarah's Grandad Eric gave her a set of dominoes. He taught her how to play the game, which she loved, and how to set up 'Domino rallies'.

Grandad Eric said, 'You stand up the dominoes, ever so carefully, one behind the other, then gently tap the first one and watch them all tumble on to each other!'

Although it was tricky to do, Sarah became very good at it and loved the 'click-clack' sound as all the dominoes collapsed!

The next day, Sarah was playing 'Domino rallies' when Jahan came round.

'Don't disturb me, Jahan! I'm very busy!' said Sarah, rather unkindly. Jahan looked so upset that Sarah felt very sad, too.

She said, 'I'm sorry I upset you, Jahan, but you have to be very careful when you build a domino rally, otherwise the dominoes topple over before you want them to, and I wish I had some more!'

'Would you like me to get mine?' said Jahan.

'Ooh, yes please!' said Sarah.

So Sarah's mum took Jahan home to get his dominoes. Ten minutes later, Sarah and Jahan were sitting side by side at the table, taking turns very gently to build an enormously long, wiggly domino rally, which looked just like a snake. They both carefully tapped the first domino – and watched them all collapse with a huge RAT-A-RAT CLATTER!

Linda Mort

My Hug-o-saurus

Tom loved drawing. One of his favourite games was 'Fantastic creatures'. He would ask Mum or Dad, or big sister Aisha, or Granny or Grandad, to sit next to him. Then Tom would get a piece of paper for each of them and his big box of crayons. Then he would say, 'Please draw a fantastic creature! I will tell you what it looks like. Listen carefully!' Then he would say something like, 'It's got a big oval head with THREE eyes and zigzag teeth!' Then his grown-up would have to draw the head exactly as Tom had described it.

Sometimes, Tom would say, 'No, Grandad! I said THREE eyes, not two!' And Grandad would have to draw another eye. Then Tom would describe the body – 'a long, wiggly, purple body with spikes' – and the rest of the creature, and his grown-up would draw just what he said. When the picture was finished, Tom would say, 'Great! That's *exactly* what it looks like! My turn now!' And his grown-up would describe a fantastic creature to Tom. Tom always listened very carefully indeed and drew exactly what he heard!

One day, Tom and his mum were playing 'Fantastic creatures' and Tom had drawn an enormous creature with a huge smile and two very long arms and a big fluffy tail, exactly as his mum had described.

'He looks as if he could give lots of hugs!' said Tom. 'I'll call him my Hug-o-saurus. I wish he could come alive!'

That night, Tom went to bed thinking about his Hug-o-saurus. Next morning, Mum had to come and wake him.

'Guess what!' said Tom, 'Hug-o-saurus came in the middle of the night, and he brought two apples, and he gave one to me and we ate them in bed!'

'Are you sure it wasn't a dream?' said Mum.

'Oh, no!' said Tom. Then Tom's mum pulled back his duvet and saw eight apple pips in the bed!

'See! I told you!' said Tom. 'And my Hug-o-saurus gave me a great big hug just before he vanished – just like this!' And Tom gave Mum a great big hug!

Linda Mort

The hedgehog song

(Sung to the tune of 'London Bridge is Falling Down')

Autumn leaves are falling down,
Falling down, falling down.
Autumn leaves are falling down,
Now it's time to hibernate!

All the hedgehogs snuffle and shuffle,
Snuffle and shuffle, snuffle and shuffle.
All the hedgehogs snuffle and shuffle,
Looking for some food.

Now they curl up in dry leaves,
In dry leaves, in dry leaves.
Now they curl up in dry leaves,
And fall fast asleep!

From time to time, they wake and nibble,
Wake and nibble, wake and nibble.
From time to time, they wake and nibble,
Then go back to sleep!

Now the Spring has come again,
Come again, come again.
Now the Spring has come again,
The hedgehogs wake and stretch!

Linda Mort

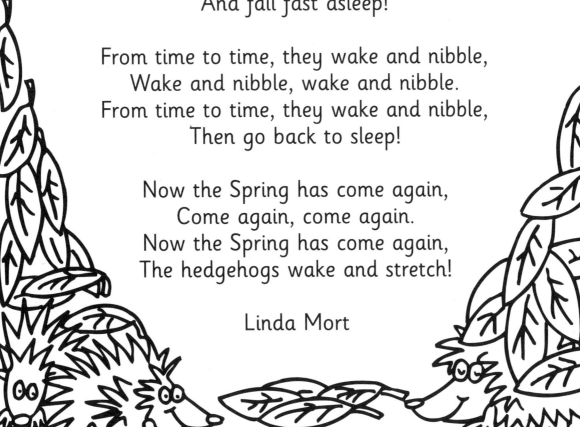

Swimming in the sea

Sticky, gooey suncream,
Rub it in, rub it in.

Run to the water...
Splash and crash!

Taste the salty water
– oh dear me!
Swim like a fish,
as fast as can be.

Is that a wave chasing me?
Yes it is, yes it is!
And I jump over it!
Splash!

Linda Mort

This is the way we are clean!

(Sung to the tune of 'Here We Go Round the Mulberry Bush')

Draw a line to join the pictures to the words in the song.

This is the way we wash our hands,
We wash our hands, we wash our hands.
This is the way we wash our hands,
So that they are clean!

This is the way we wash our face,
We wash our face, we wash our face.
This is the way we wash our face,
So that we are clean!

This is the way we wash our hair,
We wash our hair, we wash our hair.
This is the way we wash our hair,
So that it is clean!

This is the way we brush our teeth,
We brush our teeth, we brush our teeth.
This is the way we brush our teeth,
So that they are clean!

Linda Mort

Read these words and draw a line to match them to the same words in the song.

face   teeth   hands   hair

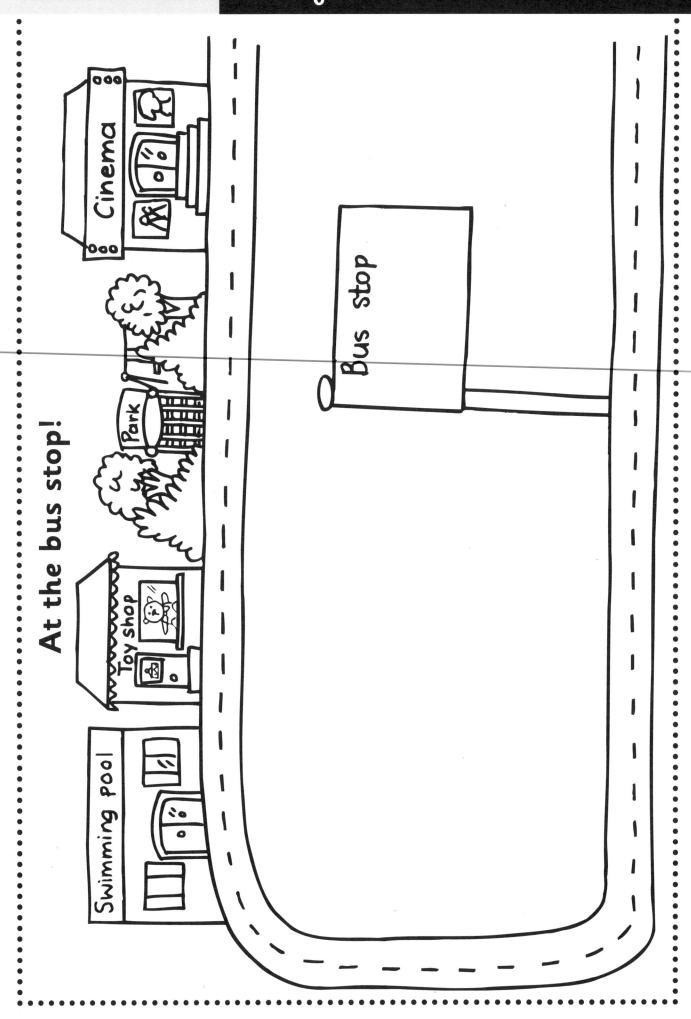

At the bus stop!

Cinema

Park

Toy shop

Swimming Pool

Bus stop

All about Divali

Alphabet letters

The straight-line family

The curvy family

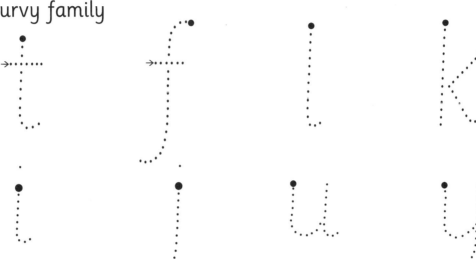

The roundy family

The down-up family

r n m h b p

How heavy is it?

Draw bags of sand in the empty pans.

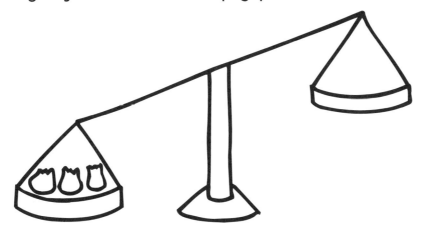

lighter

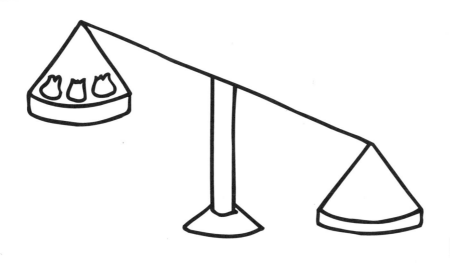

heavier

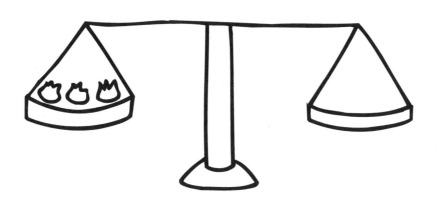

balanced

Shapes in the sand

A windy day

Clever Gulliver

Draw tiny buildings and other things that the giant Gulliver saw in the land of Lilliput.

My puppets

Cut out these finger puppets, roll them into cylinders and secure with sticky tape.

How to build a barbecue

Read these instructions out loud together with a grown-up, pointing to each word, one at a time. Then build your barbecue with toy bricks.

Instructions

Put three bricks in a row.
Put three more bricks on top.
Put three more bricks on top.

Put three bricks one on top
of the other, at each side.
Put your rack and tray on top.

Diagram

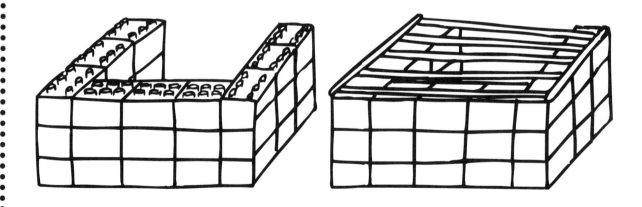

Festivals and their seasons

Draw a line to match the festivals to their seasons.

Divali

Spring

Easter

Summer

Hanukkah

Autumn

Chinese Dragon
Boat Festival

Winter

Make a telescope

Colour and decorate this telescope. Cut it out, roll it and secure it with sticky tape. Use it to play 'I spy' with a friend.

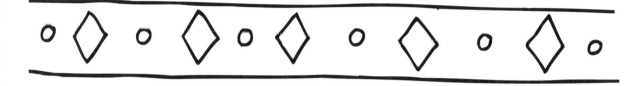

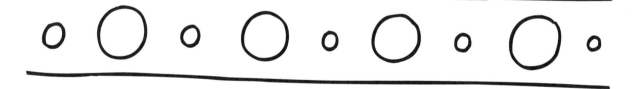

Delivery sheet

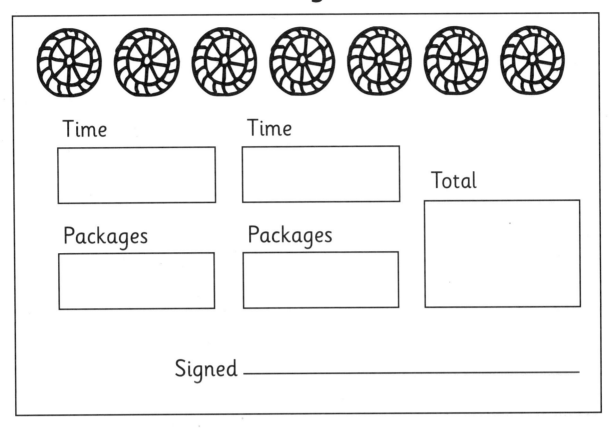

Time

Time

Total

Packages

Packages

Signed _____

Time

Time

Total

Packages

Packages

Signed _____

The 'Almost Snap!' game

Cut out these pictures. Take them into the garden and say, 'Almost Snap!' when you find the real thing.

Parents should carry babies like this...

Cut out the pictures of the animal babies and stick them in the correct positions to show them being carried.

Are you thirsty?

Write each person's name in a rectangle and draw a line in three of the tumblers to show how much water they had. Who had no water?

My photo frame

Decorate this frame, cut it out and stick it on a sheet of card. Then stick a photograph in the middle.

Pretty patterns

Draw patterns on these curtains, clothes and the table-cloth.

What could it be?

Write in the rectangles what you think each black shape could be.

Paper snakes

Decorate this part of a snake, cut it out and stick it on to your friends' snakes. Together, draw and cut out a head and stick it on to your very long snake.

Paper snakes

BASS GUITAR PLAYING

INTERMEDIATE GRADES

Grade Three to Grade Five

Compiled by

Alan J Brown & Tony Skinner

on behalf of

The Specialists in Guitar Education

RGT®

Registry of Guitar Tutors

www.RGT.org

British Library Cataloguing in Publication Data

Brown, Alan J & Skinner, Tony
Bass Guitar Playing – Intermediate Grades

ISBN 1-898466-72-6

Published in Great Britain by

Registry Mews, 11 to 13 Wilton Road, Bexhill, East Sussex, TN40 1HY

Music and text typesetting by

Printed and bound in Great Britain

v.20111220

Contents

INTRODUCTION

This handbook is primarily intended to give advice and information to candidates taking the Grades 3, 4 and 5 examinations in Bass Guitar Playing. However, the information will undoubtedly be helpful to all bass guitarists, whether they intend to take the examination or not.

The handbook aims to aid the establishment of good musical and technical foundations. Although it can be used for independent study, it is best used as a supplement to individual or group tuition, and is not designed to replace the need for guidance from an experienced teacher.

To use this handbook to best effect it is essential that the general introductions to each chapter are carefully studied, in addition to the relevant sections for each grade.

In order to illustrate the information about scales, arpeggios and other bass patterns as clearly as possible to all players, regardless of experience, the book uses the Registry of Guitar Tutors' unique *Guitarograph* system.

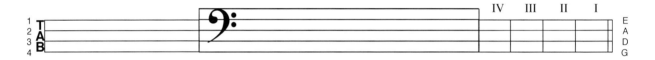

The *Guitarograph* uses a combination of tablature, traditional notation and fingerboard diagram. These are explained individually below:

(1) Tablature

The horizontal lines represent the strings in descending order, as indicated. The numbers on the string lines refer to the frets at which the left-hand

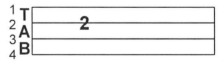

fingers should press. This example means: play on string 2 at fret 2.

(2) Bass clef notation

The lines and spaces of the bass clef indicate notes as follows:

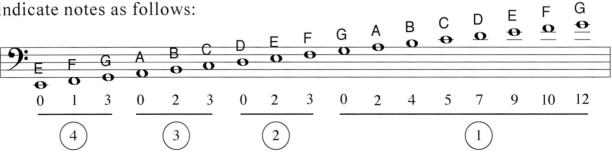

A sharp (♯) before a note *raises* its pitch by a semitone, i.e. the note is played one fret higher.

A flat (♭) before a note *lowers* its pitch by a semitone, i.e. the note is played one fret lower.

In the example, the circled numbers at the bottom refer to a string on which each note could be played. The other numbers refer to the fret on that string at which the note is to be found. The same note could be played on another string – so it is important to always refer to either the tablature or fingerboard diagram.

(3) Fingerboard diagram

Each horizontal line represents a string. The vertical lines represent the frets. Each fret is given a number in Roman numerals. Numbers on the horizontal lines indicate the left-hand finger to be used.

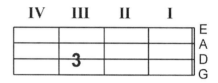

Play at the 3rd fret of the D string using the 3rd finger.

Guitarograph

All three previous methods are ways of illustrating the same information. In this Handbook all are used in combination, using the *guitarograph*. This leaves no doubt as to what is required.

This example therefore means:
play the note C (notation),
play string 3 at fret 3 (tablature),
use finger 3 (fingerboard diagram).

Above each *guitarograph* is a scale or arpeggio spelling. This lists the letter names of the notes to be played, together with their *interval numbers*.

The interval numbers refer to the position of the notes in comparison to the major scale with the same starting note. For example:

C Major Scale

note names:	C	D	E	F	G	A	B	C
interval number:	1	2	3	4	5	6	7	8

Alternative positions and fingerings

When using the *guitarograph*, please remember that the *note names* given are definitive, that is, they cannot be changed. However, on the bass guitar, it is possible to play a note at more than one position on the fingerboard. For example, the note C given in the previous examples can also be played at the same pitch on string 4 at fret 8. This is called an alternative *position*. Nevertheless, you should normally play notes at the points indicated by the tablature and fingerboard diagrams, unless you are advised otherwise by your teacher. The reason can be shown by an example: in earlier grades, open string notes are often recommended to facilitate ease of playing; at higher grades, fretted notes are used more often to facilitate transpositional fingering of scales and patterns.

It is also possible to play the scales and patterns with fingers other than those indicated. There are various reasons why other fingers might be chosen. For example, on the bass guitar a major consideration is the size of a players hands, and the ability to stretch over several frets. The fingering given in this handbook, although carefully chosen as being generally suitable, are only one possible recommended suggestion.

Please note that in the examinations you are allowed to use any alternative systematic fingering, *provided that this produces a good musical result.*

This handbook has been designed with the standard 4 string bass guitar in mind, however the use of 5 or 6 string basses in the examination is perfectly acceptable.

Tuning

The use of an electronic tuner or other tuning aid, prior to or at the start of the examination, is permitted; candidates should be able to make any further adjustments, if required during the examination, unaided. The examiner will provide an open string note to tune to when requested.

For examination purposes the bass guitar should be tuned to Standard Concert Pitch, that is A=440Hz. Candidates who normally adopt any other tuning should alter their tuning to Standard Pitch for the examination.

SECTION 1
Scales & Arpeggios

A maximum of 15 marks may be awarded in this section of the examination, with the emphasis on accurate, clear and even playing.

The scales and arpeggios required for each grade are listed on the following pages. The examiner will choose a selection of these and ask you to play them from memory. They should be played ascending and descending without a pause and without repeating the top note.

Choose a tempo at which you feel confident and maintain this evenly throughout – evenness and clarity are more important than speed for its own sake.

The choice of scales for Grade Three is based on the *marker dot system*. The majority of bass guitars have marker dots on frets 3, 5 and 7, therefore scales have been chosen to start on these frets on either the E string or the A string. This avoids open strings and gives a good grounding in easily located scale patterns which can later be moved around the fingerboard giving access to all keys. For Grade Four and above, scale and arpeggio positions have been chosen to avoid open strings, so making the patterns readily transpositional.

Left-hand technique

Press the tips of the left-hand fingers as close to the frets as possible. This minimises both buzzes and the amount of pressure required, enabling you to play with a lighter, clearer, and hence more fluent, touch.

Try to keep all the left-hand fingers close to the fingerboard and have them hovering, ready to press, as this reduces the amount of movement required. Always have the left-hand fingers correctly spaced and ready in position before you begin to play.

Right-hand technique

You are free to use either your fingers or a plectrum for these examinations.

If you use a plectrum, alternate downstrokes with upstrokes. Grip the plectrum between the index finger and thumb, but be careful not to grip it too tightly as excessive gripping pressure can lead to muscular tension in the right hand and arm. Position the pick so that its point is about a half a centimetre beyond the fingertip. If too much of the plectrum extends beyond the finger a lack of control will result as it will flap around when striking the strings – this would consequently reduce fluency and accuracy.

If you choose to use your fingers, alternate between the index finger and middle finger, ensuring that each finger

7

produces the same quality of sound. Keep your fingers close to the strings. The thumb may be rested on the E string whilst playing higher strings.

The *rest stroke* should be used for the majority of the time. To achieve the best results, rest your finger (either index or middle) on the string you wish to play. Pull towards the next lower string and when you have sufficient tension release the string, allowing the finger to fall onto the next lower string. The more tension you put on the string (i.e. the harder you pull before you release) the louder the note produced. Try to avoid pressing the string into the guitar body or pulling it away. The best results are achieved by creating a *walking* effect – alternating the index and middle fingers.

For the purposes of the exam, volume should be of a medium strength. Loud enough to be clear and firm, but comfortable to play.

GRADE THREE

Scales

The following one octave scales should be played ascending and descending from memory:

Major, Natural Minor, Pentatonic Minor and Blues in the keys of G, A, B, C, D, E.

Examples are given starting on G and C – showing the patterns for scales starting on the E string and the A string respectively. For the other scales required refer to the chart below detailing the starting string and fret for each key.

key	G	A	B	C	D	E
starting string	E	E	E	A	A	A
starting fret	3	5	7	3	5	7

G Major

G	A	B	C	D	E	F♯	G
1	2	3	4	5	6	7	8

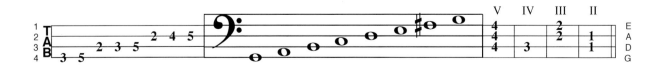

C Major

C	D	E	F	G	A	B	C
1	2	3	4	5	6	7	8

G Natural Minor

G	A	B♭	C	D	E♭	F	G
1	2	♭3	4	5	♭6	♭7	8

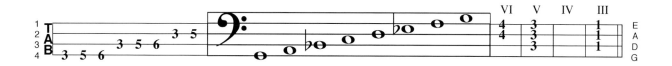

C Natural Minor

C	D	E♭	F	G	A♭	B♭	C
1	2	♭3	4	5	♭6	♭7	8

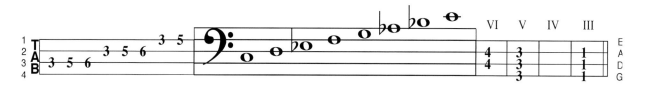

G Pentatonic Minor

G	B♭	C	D	F	G
1	♭3	4	5	♭7	8

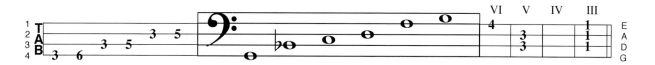

C Pentatonic Minor

C	E♭	F	G	B♭	C
1	♭3	4	5	♭7	8

G Blues

G	Bb	C	Db	D	F	G
1	b3	4	b5	5	b7	8

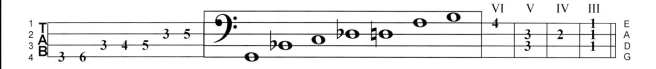

C Blues

C	Eb	F	Gb	G	Bb	C
1	b3	4	b5	5	b7	8

Arpeggios

The following one octave arpeggios should be played ascending and descending from memory:

Major, Minor, Major 7th, Minor 7th and Dominant 7th in all keys.

Examples are given starting on G and C – showing the patterns for arpeggios starting on the E string and the A string respectively. For the other arpeggios required refer to the chart below detailing the starting string and fret for each arpeggio.

arpeggio	F#/Gb	G	G#/Ab	A	A#/Bb	B	C	C#/Db	D	D#/Eb	E	F
starting string	E	E	E	E	E	A	A	A	A	A	A	A
starting fret	2	3	4	5	6	2	3	4	5	6	7	8

G Major

G	B	D	G
R	3	5	R

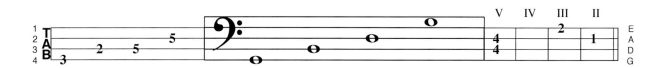

10

C Major

C	E	G	C
R	3	5	R

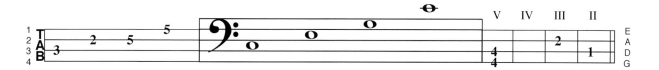

G Minor

G	B♭	D	G
R	♭3	5	R

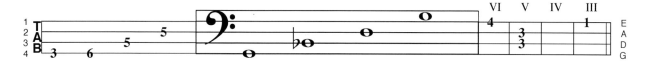

C Minor

C	E♭	G	C
R	♭3	5	R

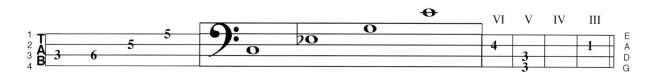

G Major 7

G	B	D	F♯	G
R	3	5	7	R

C Major 7

C	E	G	B	C
R	3	5	7	R

11

G Minor 7

G   B♭   D   F   G
R   ♭3   5   ♭7   R

C Minor 7

C   E♭   G   B♭   C
R   ♭3   5   ♭7   R

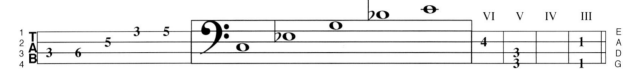

G Dominant 7

G   B   D   F   G
R   3   5   ♭7   R

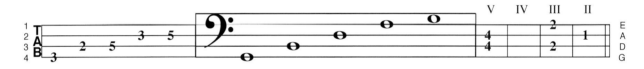

C Dominant 7

C   E   G   B♭   C
R   3   5   ♭7   R

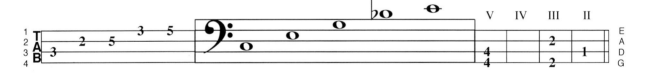

GRADE FOUR

Scales

Candidates should be able to play all scales listed in previous grades. In addition, the following one octave scales should be played ascending and descending in TWO different fingerboard positions, from memory:

Major, Natural Minor, Pentatonic Minor and Blues in the keys of A to F# inclusive.

Examples are given starting on C – showing the patterns for scales starting on the E string in the two positions. For the other scales required refer to the chart below which details the starting string and fret for each key.

key	A	A#/B♭	B	C	C#/D♭	D	D#/E♭	E	F	F#/G♭
starting string	E	E	E	E	E	E	E	E	E	E
starting fret	5	6	7	8	9	10	11	12	13	14

C Major

C	D	E	F	G	A	B	C
1	2	3	4	5	6	7	8

C Natural Minor

C	D	E♭	F	G	A♭	B♭	C
1	2	♭3	4	5	♭6	♭7	8

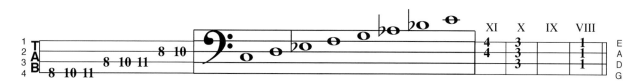

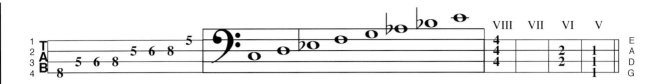

C Pentatonic Minor

C	Eb	F	G	Bb	C
1	b3	4	5	b7	8

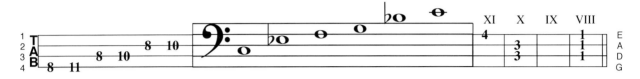

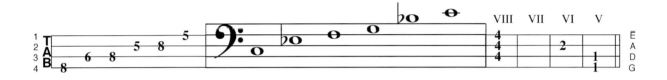

C Blues

C	Eb	F	Gb	G	Bb	C
1	b3	4	b5	5	b7	8

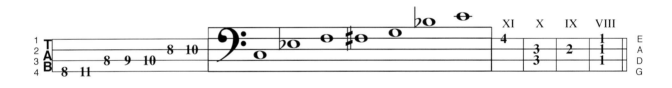

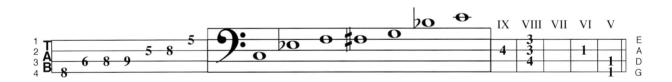

14

Arpeggios

Candidates should be able to play all arpeggios listed in previous grades. In addition, the following one octave arpeggios should be played ascending and descending in TWO different fingerboard positions, from memory:

Major, Minor, Major 7th, Minor 7th and Dominant 7th with root notes of A to F# inclusive.

Examples are given starting on C – showing the patterns for arpeggios starting on the E string. For the other arpeggios required refer to the chart in the scales section which details the starting string and fret for each arpeggio.

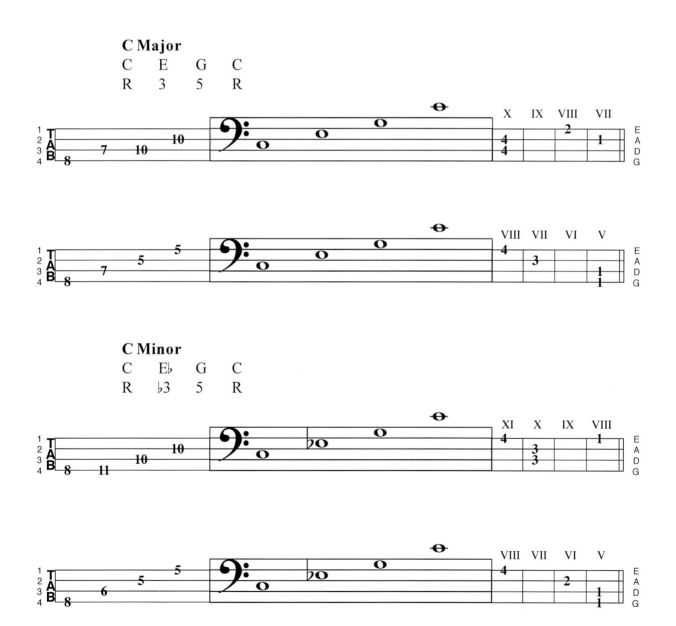

C Major 7

C	E	G	B	C
R	3	5	7	R

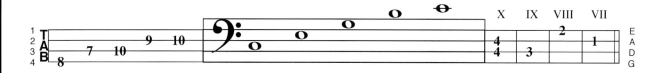

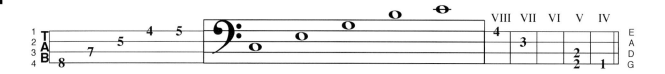

C Minor 7

C	E♭	G	B♭	C
R	♭3	5	♭7	R

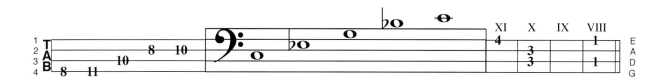

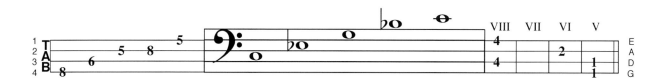

C Dominant 7

C	E	G	B♭	C
R	3	5	♭7	R

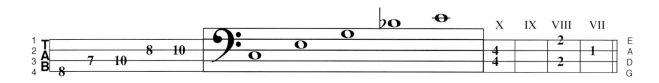

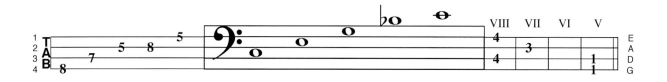

GRADE FIVE

Scales

Candidates should be able to play all scales listed in previous grades. In addition, the following one octave scales should be played ascending and descending in THREE different fingerboard positions, from memory:

Major, Natural Minor, Pentatonic Minor and Blues in the keys of B to F# inclusive.

Examples are given starting on C – showing the patterns for the three positions. The first two positions begin on the E string, the third begins on the A string. For the other keys required refer to the chart below which details the starting string and fret for each key.

key	B	C	C#/Db	D	D#/Eb	E	F	F#/Gb
E string (shapes 1 and 2) starting fret	7	8	9	10	11	12	13	14
A string (shape 3) starting fret	2	3	4	5	6	7	8	9

C Major

C	D	E	F	G	A	B	C
1	2	3	4	5	6	7	8

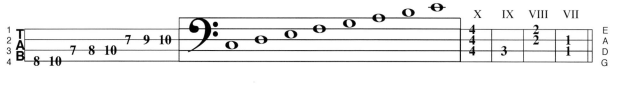

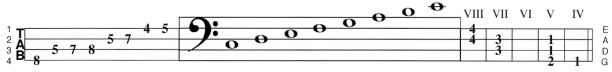

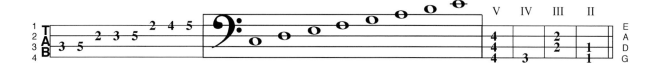

17

C Natural Minor

C	D	E♭	F	G	A♭	B♭	C
1	2	♭3	4	5	♭6	♭7	8

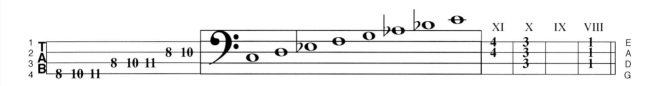

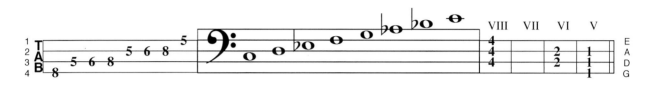

C Pentatonic Minor

C	E♭	F	G	B♭	C
1	♭3	4	5	♭7	8

18

C Blues

C	E♭	F	G♭	G	B♭	C
1	♭3	4	♭5	5	♭7	8

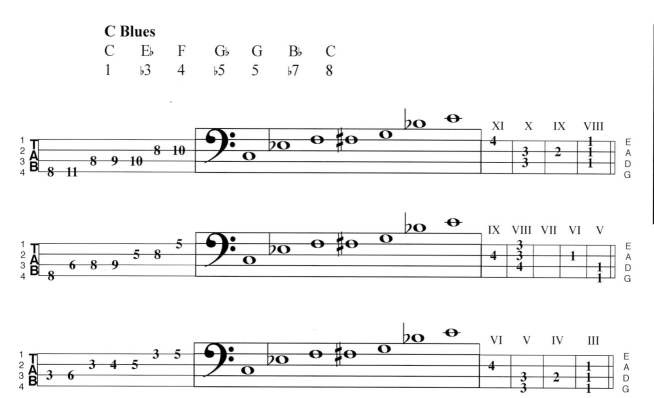

Arpeggios

Candidates should be able to play all arpeggios listed in previous grades. In addition, the following one octave arpeggios should be played ascending and descending in TWO different fingerboard positions, from memory:

Sus 4th, Major 6th, Minor 6th, Major 7th, Minor 7th and Dominant 7th with root notes of A to F♯ inclusive.

Examples are given starting on C – showing the patterns for arpeggios starting on the E string. For the other arpeggios required refer to the chart below which details the starting string and fret for each arpeggio.

arpeggio	A	A♯/B♭	B	C	C♯/D♭	D	D♯/E♭	E	F	F♯/G♭
starting string	E	E	E	E	E	E	E	E	E	E
starting fret	5	6	7	8	9	10	11	12	13	14

C Sus 4

C	F	G	C
R	4	5	R

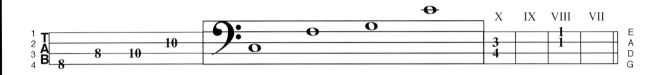

C Major 6

C	E	G	A	C
R	3	5	6	R

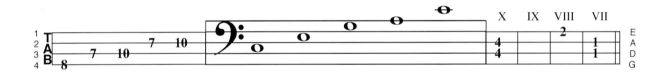

C Minor 6

C	E♭	G	A	C
R	♭3	5	6	R

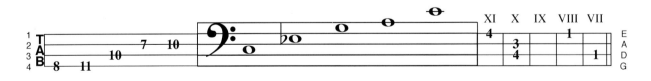

C Major 7

C	E	G	B	C
R	3	5	7	R

C Minor 7

C	E♭	G	B♭	C
R	♭3	5	♭7	R

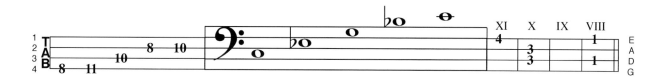

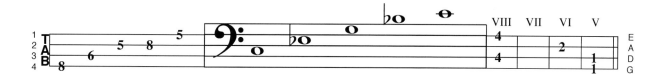

C Dominant 7

C	E	G	B♭	C
R	3	5	♭7	R

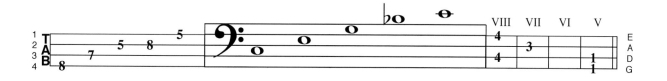

SECTION 2
Bass Patterns

A maximum of 24 marks may be awarded in this section of the examination.

The candidate should select two bass patterns from the four examples of the relevant grade given on the following pages. The candidate will then be shown a chord progression for one of the choices. The chosen bass pattern should be played over this sequence, transposing it for each chord. The chord progression should be played through three times. The second and third time the candidate may vary the pattern rhythmically and/or melodically, but should still follow the chord sequence and keep within the musical style. A broad indication of the general style and suggested speed is given with each bass pattern. Normally only one performance is required but, at the examiner's discretion, the candidate may be requested to play the second bass pattern over another chord sequence.

Marks will be awarded in this section for accuracy of pitch, security of timing and creativity.

The bass patterns and chords used in each sequence will be based on the requirements for Sections 1 and 3 of the relevant grade. The following pages show the bass patterns in the key of C major or C minor, followed by examples of the type of progression to be expected in a variety of keys. Above the chord progression is the riff as it should be played for each chord. This is shown in both standard notation and tablature.

Please note that in the examination candidates will be shown only a chord sequence. The bass pattern that is notated over each chord in this handbook is shown only to ensure clarity and to facilitate the learning process. Such notation will NOT appear on the examination chord chart. Above each bass pattern is given a broad indication of style together with a suggested metronome marking. These are a general guide to playing and some flexibility in interpretation is allowed.

A page of practice charts will be found for each grade. Candidates should practice playing the bass pattern over all the chords to be expected, in a variety of chord progressions, rather than merely practicing the examples provided in this handbook.

GRADE THREE

The chord sequence may contain chords in any key, but will be limited to the following types:

Major, Minor, Major 7th, Minor 7th and Dominant 7th.

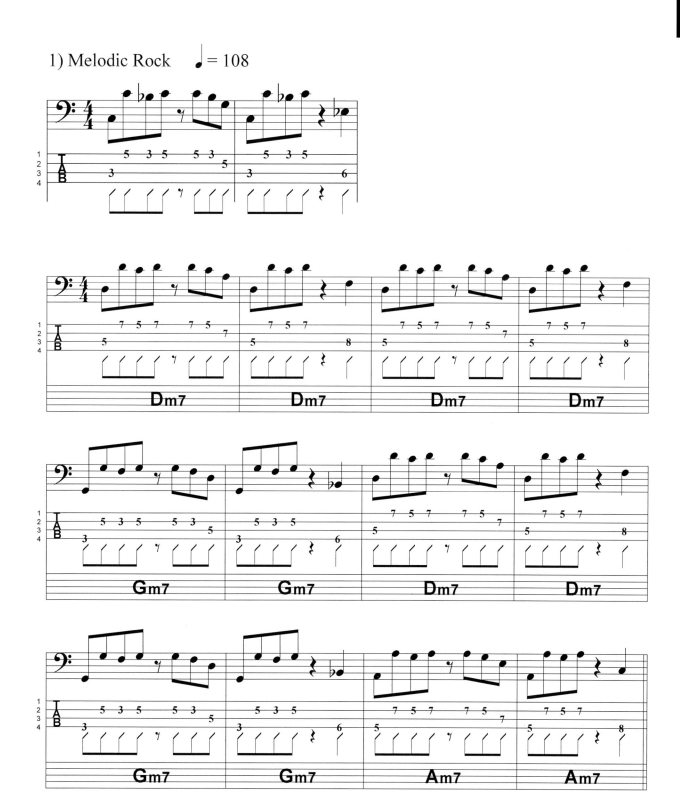

23

2) Slow Funk   ♩ = 80

3) R&B   ♩ = 120

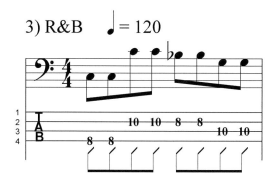

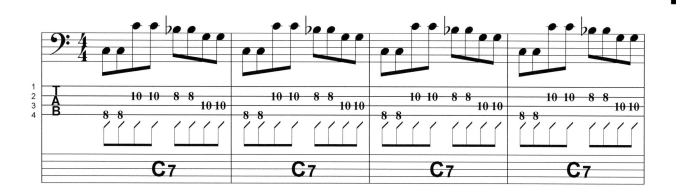

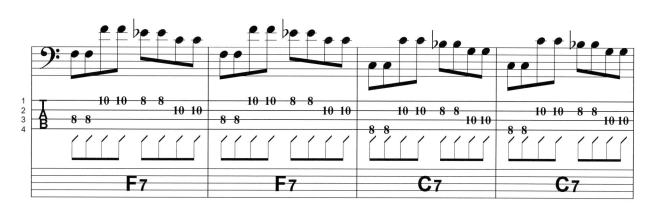

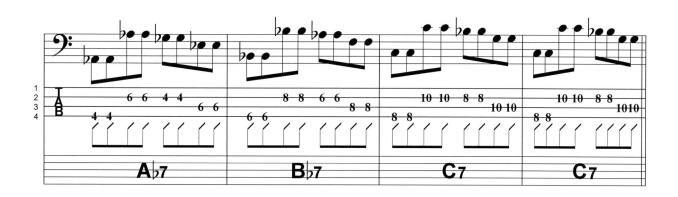

4) Ballad   ♩ = 92

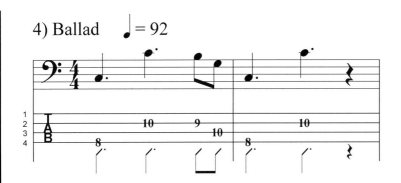

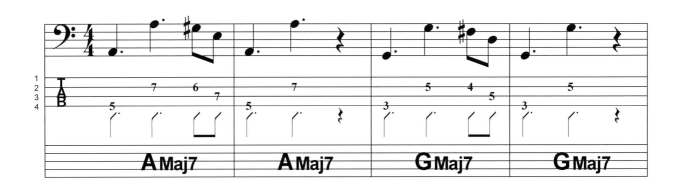

A Maj7   A Maj7   G Maj7   G Maj7

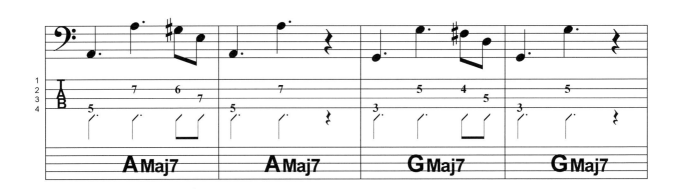

A Maj7   A Maj7   G Maj7   G Maj7

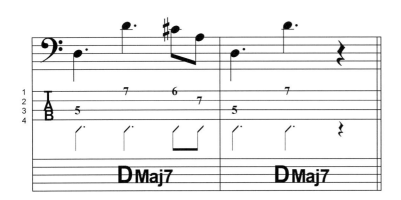

D Maj7   D Maj7

The chord charts below are similar to those presented to the candidate in the examination (i.e. without notation and tablature). They are given here as an aid to practice, with one progression for each bass pattern. Candidates are encouraged to practice each bass pattern over as many different chord progressions as possible.

1) Melodic Rock

| Em7 | Em7 | Em7 | Em7 | Am7 | Am7 |

| Em7 | Em7 | Am7 | Am7 | Bm7 | Bm7 |

2) Slow Funk

| E7 | E7 | D7 | A7 |

| E7 | E7 | D7 | B7 |

3) R & B

| D7 | D7 | D7 | D7 | G7 | G7 |

| D7 | D7 | B♭7 | C7 | D7 | D7 |

4) Ballad

| B Maj7 | B Maj7 | A Maj7 | A Maj7 | B Maj7 |

| B Maj7 | A Maj7 | A Maj7 | E Maj7 | E Maj7 |

GRADE FOUR

The chord sequence may contain chords in any key, but will be limited to the following types: Major, Minor, Major 7th , Minor 7th and Dominant 7th.

1) Minor Jazz   ♩ = 176

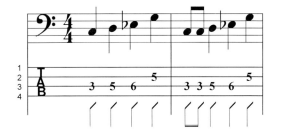

Although written in 4/4 for ease of reading, this piece should be played with a 12/8 feel in order to achieve an authentic jazz style.

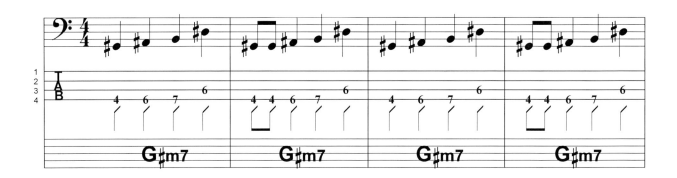

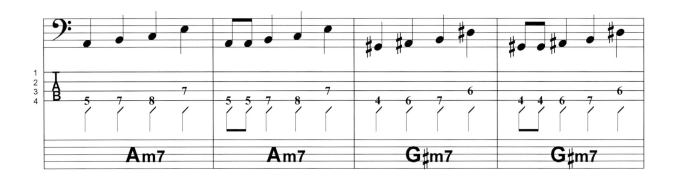

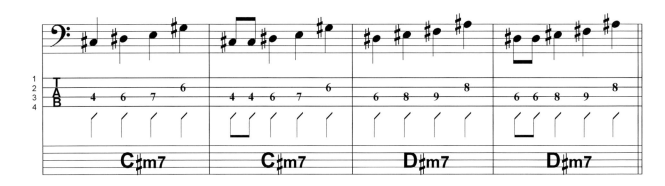

2) Rhythm & Blues ♩ = 120

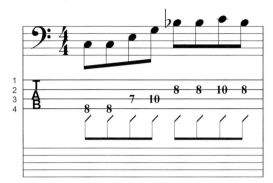

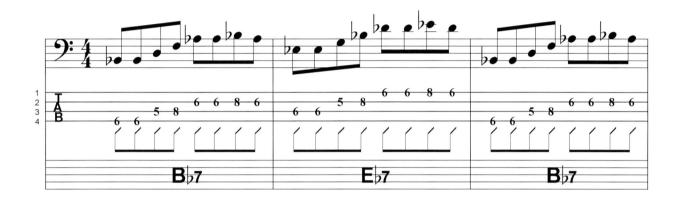

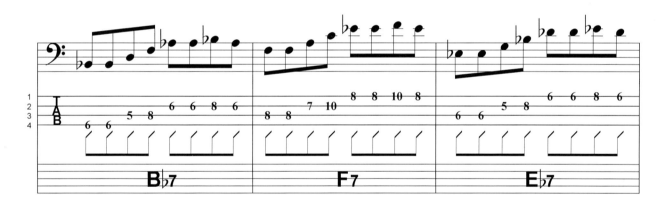

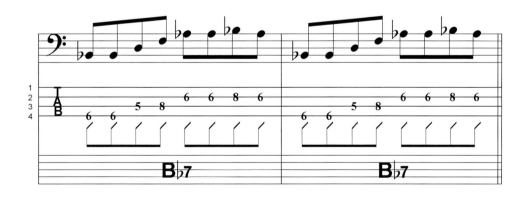

3) Light Rock ♩ = 66

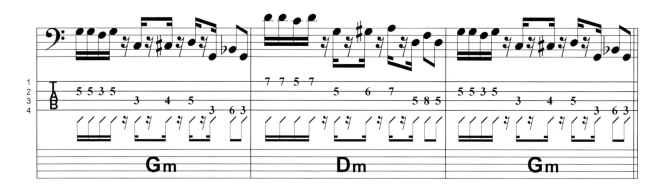

30

4) Rock Blues ♩. = 100

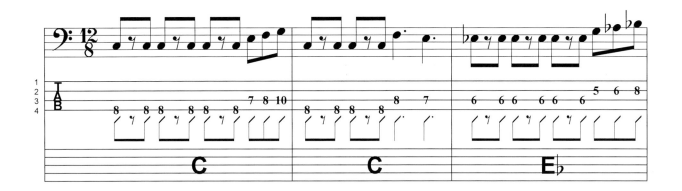

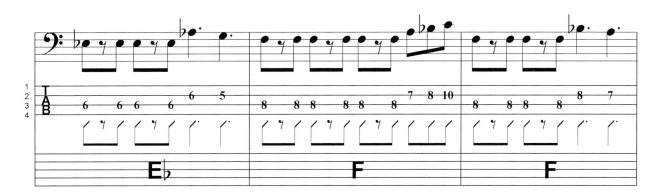

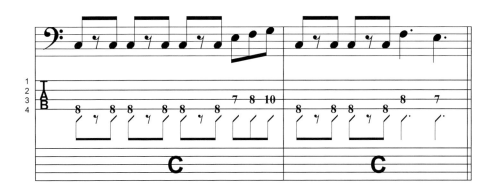

The chord charts below are similar to those presented to the candidate in the examination (i.e. without notation and tablature). They are given here as an aid to practice, with one progression for each bass pattern. Candidates are encouraged to practice each bass pattern over as many different chord progressions as possible.

1) Minor Jazz

| F♯m7 | F♯m7 | F♯m7 | F♯m7 | Gm7 | Gm7 |

| F♯m7 | F♯m7 | Bm7 | Bm7 | C♯m7 | C♯m7 |

2) Rhythm & Blues

| A♭7 | D♭7 | A♭7 | A♭7 |

| E♭7 | D♭7 | A♭7 | A♭7 |

3) Light Rock

| Fm | Fm | B♭m |

| Fm | Cm | Fm |

4) Rock Blues

| B♭ | B♭ | D♭ | D♭ |

| E♭ | E♭ | B♭ | B♭ |

GRADE FIVE

The chord sequence may contain the following chord types:

Major, Minor, Major 7th , Minor 7th and Dominant 7th in any key.

Sus 4th, Major 6th and Minor 6th with root notes of A to F# inclusive.

From Grade Five candidates should be able to play *slurs*, often referred to as the *hammer on* and the *pull off*. Details concerning this technique will be found in the Grade Five part of the Musicianship section in this Handbook.

Where a bass pattern consists of two bars, and the chord changes after only one bar of the pattern, then only the first bar of the pattern should be played.

1) Soul Pop ♩ = 96

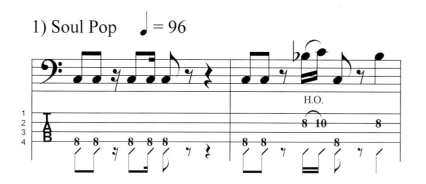

Where a bass pattern consists of two bars, and the chord changes after only one bar of the pattern, then only the first bar of the pattern should be played.

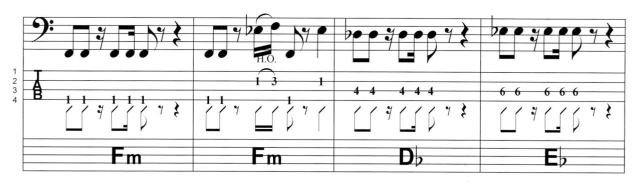

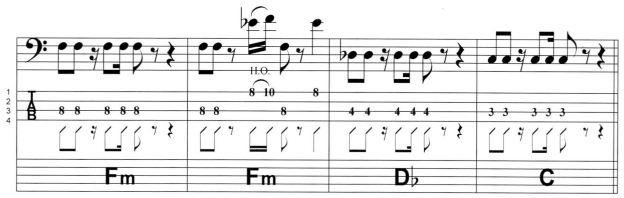

33

2) R & B ♩ = 152

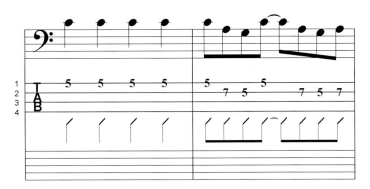

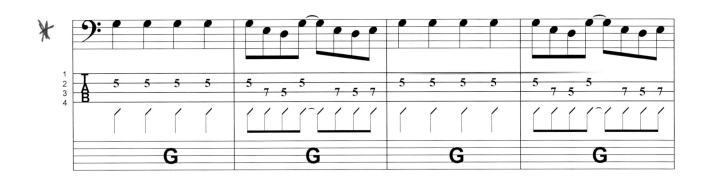

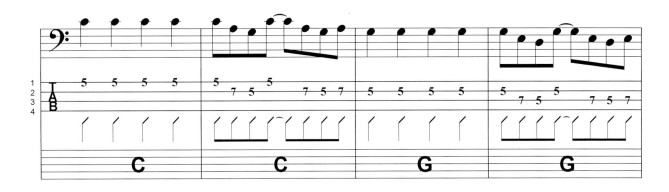

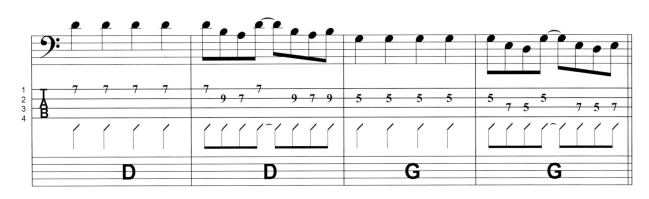

3) Minor Rock ♩ = 132

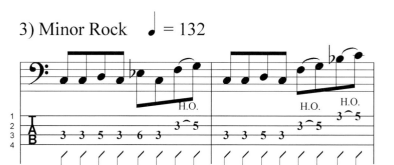

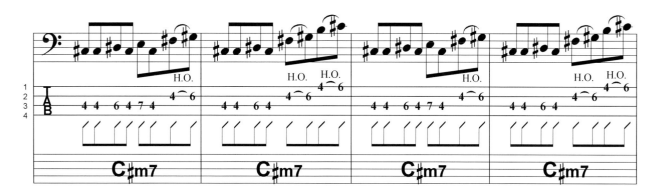

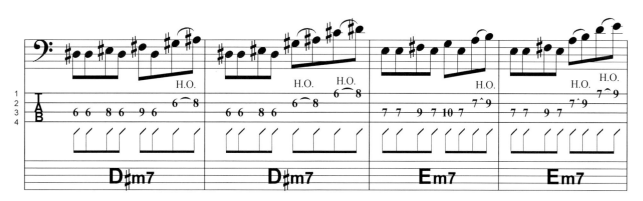

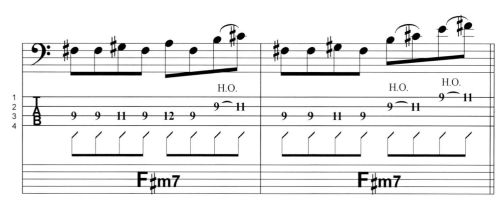

4) Indie-pop ♩=112

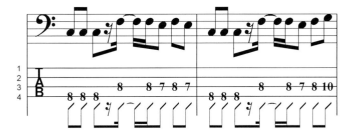

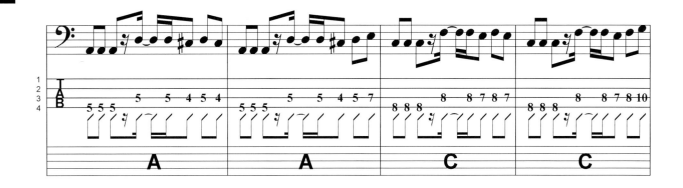

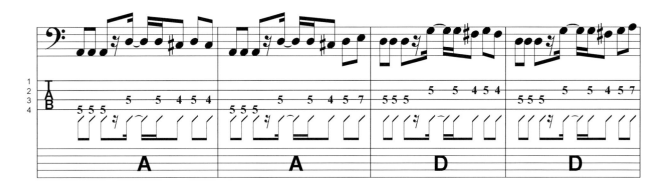

The chord charts below are similar to those presented to the candidate in the examination (i.e. without notation and tablature). They are given here as an aid to practice, with one progression for each bass pattern. Candidates are encouraged to practice each bass pattern over as many different chord progressions as possible.

1) Soul Pop

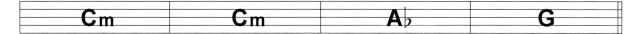

2) R & B

3) Minor Rock

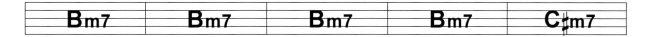

4) Indie Pop

SECTION 3
Performance

A maximum of 36 marks may be awarded in this section of the examination.

The candidate will be shown a chord sequence containing chords detailed for each grade on the following pages. The examiner will play through the sequence once on guitar (live or recorded) for the candidate to hear. The examiner will then play the sequence a further three times and the candidate should improvise an appropriate bass line over the chords.

At the examiner's discretion, a second sequence may be given in a different style over which the candidate should again improvise an appropriate bass line after having heard the sequence once.

Marks will be awarded in this section for accuracy of pitch, security of timing, rhythmic inventiveness and creativity, and at higher grades, also for fluency, melodic shaping and stylistic interpretation. Some examples of the type of sequence to be expected are shown for each grade on the following pages.

Chord Symbols

In the chord progressions, a lone upper case letter refers to a major chord and a letter followed by a lower case 'm' refers to a minor chord. An upper case letter followed by a '7' refers to a dominant seventh chord, whilst 'm7' and 'Maj7' refer to minor seventh and major seventh respectively. 'm6' after a chord letter indicates a minor 6th, whilst a lone '6' refers to a major 6th. A suspended 4th chord is abreviated to 'sus4'

For example:

D = D Major	D7 = D Dominant 7th	Dm = D Minor	Dm7 = D Minor 7th	D Maj7 = D Major 7th

Dm6 = D Minor 6th	D6 = D Major 6th	Dsus4 = D Suspended 4th

Split Bars

When two (or more) chords appear in a single bar this is known as a split bar. Dots (or diagonal lines) after chords can be used to indicate the division of the bar: the chord symbol representing one beat and each dot representing another beat. However, if no dots are present it can be assumed that the bar is divided evenly between the chords.

GRADE THREE

The chord sequence may contain some of the following chords:

Major, Minor, Major 7th , Minor 7th and Dominant 7th in any key.

At this grade the candidate is expected to be fluent in playing the root, third and fifth of each chord and should demonstrate ability in incorporating major, minor and dominant sevenths *when musically appropriate.* However, candidates should be careful not to 'overplay': the use of too many arpeggio notes could lead to a bass line which sounds too busy; candidates should not neglect the importance of demonstrating an understanding of musical 'feel' and style.

Some examples of the type of chart that may be presented at this grade are given below. Note that at this grade the time signature is limited to ¾ ⁴₄ or ⁶₈ time and there will be only one chord per bar.

During the first playing of the sequence by the examiner, candidates should listen carefully to the way the chords are played in order to choose an appropriate style of bass line.

(i)   Soulful and not too fast

| $\frac{4}{4}$ | A♭ | Fm | Cm7 | Cm7 | A♭ | Fm | D♭ | E♭7 |

(ii) In a ballad style

| $\frac{3}{4}$ | E♭Maj7 | Fm | Cm | B♭ | E♭Maj7 | Gm | Fm | B♭7 |

(iii) Fairly slow with a bluesy feel

| $\frac{6}{8}$ | F♯m | E | D | E | F♯m | E | Bm7 | C♯m7 |

(iv) With movement

| $\frac{4}{4}$ | G | D | Am | CMaj7 | Em | Bm | C | D7 |

39

GRADE FOUR

The chord sequence may contain some of the following chords:

Major, Minor, Major 7th , Minor 7th and Dominant 7th in any key.

At this grade the candidate is expected to be fluent in playing the root, third, fifth and seventh of each chord *when musically appropriate*. However, candidates should be careful not to 'overplay': the use of too many arpeggio notes could lead to a bass line which sounds too busy; candidates should not neglect the importance of demonstrating an understanding of musical 'feel' and style.

Some examples of the type of chart that may be presented at this grade are given below.

Note that at this grade the time signature is limited to $\frac{3}{4}$ $\frac{4}{4}$ or $\frac{6}{8}$ time and there will be up to two chords per bar.

During the first playing of the sequence by the examiner, the candidate should listen carefully to the way the chords are played in order to choose an appropriate style of bass line.

(i)   Light and fairly up-tempo

| $\frac{3}{4}$ | B♭ | B♭Maj7 | E♭Maj7 | E♭Maj7 | Dm7 | Dm7 | Gm7 | F7 |

(ii) Moderately slow with feeling

| $\frac{6}{8}$ | B | G♯m7 | G♯m7 | F♯ | B | D♯m7 | D♯m7 | EMaj7 |

(iii) Bright and lively

| $\frac{4}{4}$ | A♭7 D♭7 | A♭7 E♭7 | D♭7 | A♭7 | D♭7 | E♭7 |

(iv) Slow and tenderly

| $\frac{3}{4}$ | Em | Am7 | CMaj7 | D | Em | Bm7 | CMaj7 | CMaj7 |

GRADE FIVE

The chord sequence may contain some of the following chords:

Major, Minor, Major 7th , Minor 7th and Dominant 7th in any key; Sus 4th, Major 6th and Minor 6th with root notes of A to F#, inclusive.

At this grade the candidate is expected to be fluent in playing the root, third, fifth and seventh of each chord *when musically appropriate*. However, candidates should be careful not to 'overplay': the use of too many arpeggio notes could lead to a bass line which sounds too busy; candidates should not neglect the importance of demonstrating an understanding of musical 'feel' and style.

Some examples of the type of chart that may be presented at this grade are given below.

Note that at this grade the time signature is limited to $\frac{3}{4}$ $\frac{4}{4}$ or $\frac{6}{8}$ time and there will be up to two chords per bar.

During the first playing of the sequence by the examiner, candidates should listen carefully to the way the chords are played in order to choose an appropriate style of bass line.

(i)   Bright and rhythmically

| $\frac{3}{4}$ GMaj7 | Am6 | C6 | Dsus4 | Bm | Em7 | Dsus4 | D ‖

(ii) Slow ballad

| $\frac{6}{8}$ Fm7 | D♭ | E♭ | C7 | Fm7 | B♭m7 | C7 | C7 ‖

(iii) Moderate swing ✓

| $\frac{4}{4}$ C6 | Am7 | C6 | Am7 | Dm6 | Dm6 | Em7. A7. | Dm7. G7. ‖

(iv) Medium blues

| $\frac{6}{8}$ E7 | A7 | E7 | B7 | D6 | E6 | Bsus4 | B7 ‖

SECTION 4
Musicianship

A maximum of 10 marks may be awarded in this section of the examination.

This section of the examination tests the candidate's knowledge of the notes being played, general music theory and conventions, the mechanism of the instrument and the technical aspects of playing it.

a) Musical knowledge

The candidate should be familiar with the notes in the scales and arpeggios required for the relevant grade (see Section 1 of this handbook). The examiner may ask the candidate to play any note on a particular string (which will be taken from the required scales). In order to establish a solid musical foundation it is important that candidates are aware of the notes they are playing rather than duplicating finger patterns.

This section also tests the candidate's knowledge of general music theory. The ability to follow musical instructions such as repeat markings, dynamics, etc. is important when performing music and the candidate may be asked to demonstrate a particular term in addition to giving its definition. Specific requirements are given for each grade on the following pages.

b) Playing the bass guitar

This section covers the optimum methods of achieving clarity and fluency, with questions relating to both left and right hand technique. Candidates should have a basic knowledge of both plectrum and finger styles irrespective of which they use. Specific requirements are given for each grade on the following pages.

c) Knowledge of the instrument

Candidates should have a good general knowledge of the mechanism of the instrument. This covers the anatomy of the bass guitar, including knowledge of the position and function of various items and familiarity with common terms used. Specific requirements are given for each grade on the following pages.

GRADE THREE

a) Notes on the fingerboard

The candidate should be able to name any note on any string up to, and including, the twelfth fret. This includes all the notes from the scales and arpeggios listed for Grade Three in Section 1 of this handbook. The examiner may ask the candidate to play a particular note on a particular string (such as "Play the note *F* on the *G* string").

At this grade the candidate should be able to explain the repeat and dynamic markings detailed below. The candidate may also be asked to demonstrate dynamics with a question such as "Play the note C first *f* then *p*", or "Play four Cs in the manner of this sign" (pointing to one of the dynamic markings).

The following chart shows all the notes on all four strings for the first twelve frets:

12	11	10	9	8	7	6	5	4	3	2	1	*fret*
E	D#/E♭	D	C#/D♭	C	B	A#/B♭	A	G#/A♭	G	F#/G♭	F	*E string*
A	G#/A♭	G	F#/G♭	F	E	D#/E♭	D	C#/D♭	C	B	A#/B♭	*A string*
D	C#/D♭	C	B	A#/B♭	A	G#/A♭	G	F#/G♭	F	E	D#/E♭	*D string*
G	F#/G♭	F	E	D#/E♭	D	C#/D♭	C	B	A#/B♭	A	G#/A♭	*G string*

Repeat marks

Passages to be repeated are indicated by two dots and a double bar line at the start and end of the particular section. (When the repeat is from the beginning of a piece the first set of dots is not always shown.)

For example:

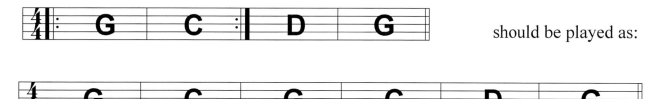

should be played as:

43

1st and 2nd time endings

Bars marked with a ⌐1.⌐ are included in the first playing but omitted on the repeat playing and replaced with the bars marked ⌐2.⌐

For example:

should be played as:

Dynamic Markings

These indicate the changes in volume to be made.

p	– play softly
f	– play strongly
—	– become louder
—	– become softer

Candidates may be given a chord sequence consisting of up to four bars with one chord per bar. The chart will contain dynamic and repeat markings. The chord sequence should be played using four root notes per bar and incorporating the performance indications. An example of the type of chart to be expected is given below.

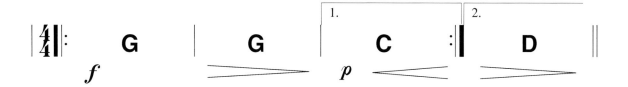

b) Playing the bass guitar

Candidates may be asked questions relating to the optimum positioning of the left-hand fingers, in particular how to obtain clear notes and avoid fret buzz. Section 1 of this handbook has details of left-hand technique, the most important aspect being keeping the left hand spread out and placing the tips of the fingers, rather than the pads, at the very edge of the frets.

Take care not to over-grip with the left-hand thumb on the back of the neck as this will cause muscle fatigue and tend to limit the freedom of the thumb to move. It is essential that the left hand thumb is allowed to move freely when changing positions. If the thumb remains static this restricts the optimum positioning of the fingers which may result in unnecessary left hand stretching and consequent loss of fluency. Also be aware that for the left-hand thumb to move freely the wrist, elbow and shoulder must be flexible and relaxed. Try to ensure that this is not inhibited by your standing or sitting position.

With regard to the right hand: plectrum strokes should alternate between down and up strokes and, in fingerstyle, index and middle fingers should alternate to facilitate fluency and speed. Section 1 of this handbook has details of right-hand technique, covering both plectrum and finger style.

In addition to answering questions, the candidate should be able to demonstrate any of the above.

c) Knowledge of the instrument

Candidates should have a good general knowledge of the bass. In particular:

i) Variations in tone achieved by changing the right hand position. For instance a brighter clearer attack will be produced when playing close to the bridge, whereas a warmer, more mellow tone is produced as you move towards the fingerboard.

ii) A practical understanding of the use of tone controls and pick-up selectors (where appropriate), to produce various tone qualities.

iii) The function of the machine heads. These are normally positioned by the headstock of the guitar. Each string has its own machine head (or turning head) which, when rotated, increases or reduces the tension exerted on that string, thereby raising or lowering its pitch. By carefully adjusting all of these the bass guitar can be brought into tune.

iv) The meaning of terms such as:

Action – the distance between the strings and the frets. This determines the ease of fretting notes.

Marker dots – the dots or blocks inlaid into the face and/or side of the fingerboard to aid in the location of certain frets. These normally include frets 3, 5, 7, 9 & 12.

The nut – a slotted piece of material (normally plastic or brass) situated at the head end of the fingerboard. The strings lie in the grooves of the nut.

The saddle – the seat upon which the string rests at the body end of the bass guitar. It is from this point that the vibrating section of the string starts.

GRADE FOUR

a) Notes on the fingerboard

Candidates should have a thorough knowledge of the requirements for Grade Three, detailed on the previous pages. Below are detailed the additional requirements for this grade.

For Grade Four, candidates should be able to name any note on any string up to, and including, the fifteenth fret. This includes all the notes from the scales and arpeggios listed for Grade Four in Section 1 of this handbook. The examiner may either name a particular string and fret and the candidate should identify this note, or ask the candidate to play a particular note on a particular string (such as "Play the note *F#* on the *G* string").

The following chart shows all the notes on all four strings for the first fifteen frets:

15	14	13	12	11	10	9	8	7	6	5	4	3	2	1 *fret*	
G	F#/G♭	F	E	D#/E♭	D	C#/D♭	C	B	A#/B♭	A	G#/A♭	G	F#/G♭	F	E
C	B	A#/B♭	A	G#/A♭	G	F#/G♭	F	E	D#/E♭	D	C#/D♭	C	B	A#/B♭	A
F	E	D#/E♭	D	C#/D♭	C	B	A#/B♭	A	G#/A♭	G	F#/G♭	F	E	D#/E♭	D
A#/B♭	A	G#/A♭	G	F#/G♭	F	E	D#/E♭	D	C#/D♭	C	B	A#/B♭	A	G#/A♭	G

Repeat and dynamic markings

In addition to the repeat and dynamic markings listed in Grade Three, candidates are expected to know the following:

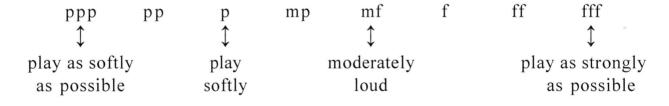

ppp	pp	p	mp	mf	f	ff	fff
↕		↕		↕			↕
play as softly as possible		play softly		moderately loud			play as strongly as possible

b) Playing the bass guitar

Candidates should have a good understanding of the techniques described in the Grade Three section. The questions asked at Grade Four will be to a greater depth. Candidates should also be able to demonstrate their answers confidently and accurately.

c) Knowledge of the instrument

Candidates should have a good knowledge of the requirements described in the Grade Three section and should be able to demonstrate a practical understanding of these topics.

In addition, candidates are expected to be able to describe the following:

Changing a string – Candidates should be aware of how to replace a string on their own instrument.

Tuning the bass guitar – Candidates should be able to explain the method they use to tune a bass guitar.

GRADE FIVE

a) Musical Knowledge

Candidates should have a thorough knowledge of the requirements for Grade Three and Grade Four, detailed on the previous pages. Below are detailed the additional requirements for this grade.

The candidate should be able to name any note on the fingerboard. The examiner may either name a particular string and fret and the candidate should identify this note, or ask the candidate to play a particular note on a particular string (such as "Play the note C on the D string").

Candidates should have a thorough knowledge of all the repeat and dynamic markings presented in the Grade Three and Grade Four sections on the previous pages.

At this grade the candidate should be able to demonstrate and name the diatonic intervals of *any* major scale

The following example shows the intervals from the C Major scale. The fingerings given are transposable to other keys.

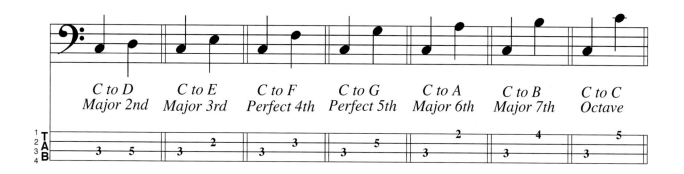

b) Playing the bass guitar

Candidates should have a thorough understanding of the information given in the Grade Three and Grade Four sections. The questions asked at Grade Five will go into greater detail. In addition, candidates should be familiar with the use of slurs.

A slur is the sounding of two or more notes from the single pick of a string. Slurs can be used to add speed to one's playing, but equally importantly to add smoothness, flow and subtlety. Candidates should be able to demonstrate ability in two type of slurs :

(a) *The Hammer-on*: A note is played, then a higher note on the same string is sounded without being picked by the right hand, rather by a hammering action with a left hand finger. For the hammered note to be clear it is important to use a certain amount of force and attack in bringing down the hammering finger. Hammer with the tip of the finger and hammer to the edge of the fret.

(b) *The Pull-off*: A note is fretted, then a lower note is sounded without being picked by the right hand, but rather by being plucked downwards by the left hand finger which was fretting the original note. For the pull-off to be clear it is important that the pressure is concentrated on the lower finger which is anchoring the string (otherwise the note may be pulled out of tune when the higher finger pulls off). The plucking action should come from the tip of the finger with a downward pulling action and not simply the lifting off of the finger into the air.

c) Knowledge of the instrument

Candidates should have a thorough understanding of the information given in the Grade Three and Grade Four sections. In addition to knowing the variations in tone achievable with the use of tone controls, candidates should be able to describe and demonstrate the difference in tone and volume produced by varying the pace and strength with which the right hand fingers pluck (or the plectrum strikes) the string.

Tuning the bass guitar

Candidates should be able to explain and demonstrate at least two methods of achieving standard relative tuning. Of the various methods, the two most common are:

a) Tuning with harmonics: Play the 5th fret harmonic on the 4th string, then play the 7th fret harmonic on the 3rd string; adjust the 3rd string until the two harmonics sound the same. Repeat for the 3rd to 2nd string and for the 2nd to 1st string.

b) The fifth fret method: Play the 5th fret of the 4th string, tune the open 3rd string to this. The 5th fret of the 3rd string is now used to tune the open 2nd string, and the 5th fret of the 2nd string is used to tune the open 1st string.

Both these methods assume you have been given an E in order to first tune your 4th string. For example, from a keyboard, guitar or tuning fork.

Aural Assessment

A maximum of 15 marks may be awarded in this section of the examination.

This section of the examination tests the aural abilities of the candidate. It consists of five sections as detailed below. Three or more sections may be tested in the examination at the discretion of the examiner, but the candidate is expected to be competent in all five.

a) Repetition of rhythms

The examiner will twice play on a single note a rhythmic pattern (examples of which are given for each grade on the following pages). The candidate should then attempt to reproduce this rhythm by either clapping or playing on any note.

b) Repetition of phrases

The candidate will be asked to look away whilst the examiner plays a four beat phrase. The phrase will be taken from one of the required scales from the appropriate grade (see Section 1 of this handbook). The candidate will be told which scale is being used, and the tonic note will be played. The examiner will play the phrase twice before the candidate makes a first attempt to reproduce the phrase. If required, the examiner will play the phrase one further time prior to the candidate's second attempt. In order to simulate circumstances which commonly occur for bass players in a band situation, the

examiner will play the phrase on the guitar or keyboard and the candidate is expected to reproduce it at any octave on the bass guitar. Examples of the type of phrase which will occur at each grade are given on the following pages.

c) Beating of time

The examiner will play a four bar phrase twice on guitar or keyboard. During the second playing the candidate should tap or clap the main pulse, accenting the first beat of the bar. An example is given for each grade on the following pages.

d) Harmony test

This section tests recognition of scale, arpeggio or chord types. The examiner will play the test on guitar or keyboard whilst the candidate looks away. Details of the requirements for each grade are given on the following pages.

e) Pitch test

This test will be played by the examiner on the candidate's bass guitar or on keyboard. In contrast to d) above, which tests a general awareness of scales, arpeggios and chords, this test is related to individual notes in the range actually being played on the bass guitar. The requirements for each grade are given on the following pages.

GRADE THREE

a) Repetition of rhythms

The examiner will twice tap or play on a single note, a four bar rhythm in either ¾ ¼ or ⅝ time. The note range will be limited to eighth notes (quavers), quarter notes (crotchets), dotted quarter notes (dotted crotchets) and half notes (minims) except for the last bar – which will contain only one long note. The candidate should then attempt to reproduce this rhythm by either clapping or playing. Some examples of the *type* of rhythm are given below. Note that the third bar is always a repeat of the first bar.

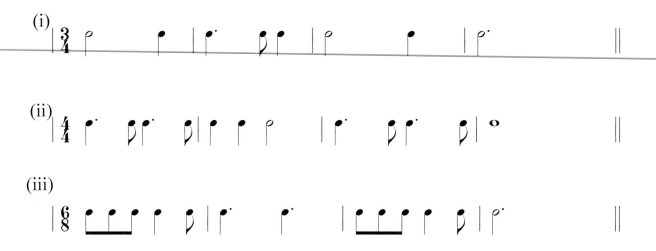

b) Repetition of phrases

The phrase given at this grade will consist of notes within a range of one octave taken from a scale listed for Grade Three in Section 1 of this handbook – the candidate will be told which scale is to be used, and the tonic note will be played. The phrase will consist of 3 quarter notes (crotchets) and 2 eighth notes (quavers). Some examples of the type of phrases are shown below.

c) Beating of time

The examiner will twice play a four bar phrase in $\frac{3}{4}$ $\frac{4}{4}$ or $\frac{6}{8}$ time, that may include dotted quarter notes (dotted crotchets) and 16th notes (semiquavers). During the second playing the candidate should tap or clap the main pulse, accenting the first beat of the bar. An example is given below.

Examiner plays:

Candidate taps:

d) Harmony tests

Whilst the candidate looks away, the examiner will play ascending and descending one of the arpeggios listed for Grade Three in Section 1 of this handbook. The candidate will then be asked to identify the nature of the arpeggio, i.e. whether it was major or minor.

e) Pitch tests

The candidate will be asked to identify any note of any one octave major scale. The examiner will first state the key and then play the tonic note, followed by any other note of the scale. The candidate should identify the second note either by interval number or by letter name. An example in the key of C major is given below.

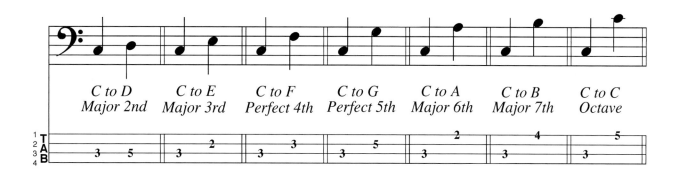

It may be easier to remember the sound of these intervals if at first each one is related to the start of a familiar tune or riff. For example, the following traditional tunes start with a perfect fourth – Amazing Grace, Auld Lang Syne, Away in a Manger.

GRADE FOUR

a) Repetition of rhythms

The examiner will twice tap or play on a single note, a four bar rhythm in either ¾ ⁴⁄₄ or ⁶⁄₈ time. The note range will be limited to 16th notes (semiquavers), eighth notes (quavers), quarter notes (crotchets), dotted quarter notes (dotted crotchets) and half notes (minims) except for the last bar – which will contain only one long note. The candidate should then attempt to reproduce this rhythm by either clapping or playing. Some examples of the type of rhythm are given below. Note that the third bar is always a repeat of the first bar.

b) Repetition of phrases

The phrase given at this grade will consist of notes within a range of one octave taken from a scale listed for Grade Four in Section 1 of this handbook – the candidate will be told which scale is to be used, and the tonic note will be played. The phrase will consist of 2 quarter notes (crotchets) and 4 eighth notes (quavers). Some examples of the type of phrases are shown below.

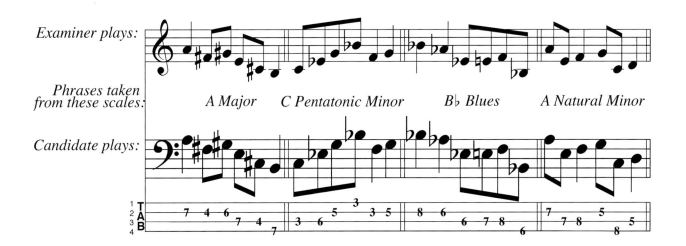

Examiner plays:

Phrases taken from these scales: *A Major*   *C Pentatonic Minor*   *B♭ Blues*   *A Natural Minor*

Candidate plays:

c) Beating of time

The examiner will twice play a four bar phrase in either ¾ ⁴⁄₄ or ⁶⁄₈ time, that may include 16th notes (semiquavers) and dotted quarter notes (dotted crotchets). After the first playing the candidate should identify the time signature.

During the second playing the candidate should tap or clap the main pulse, accenting the first beat of each bar. An example is given below.

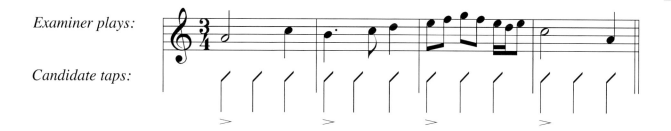

Examiner plays:

Candidate taps:

d) Harmony tests

Whilst the candidate looks away, the examiner will twice play either a Major 7th, Minor 7th or Dominant 7th chord.

The candidate will be asked to identify the type of chord played.

e) Pitch tests

The examiner will play an interval of a 3rd or a 7th in any key, sounding the notes separately. The candidate should

identify whether the interval was major or minor. For example:

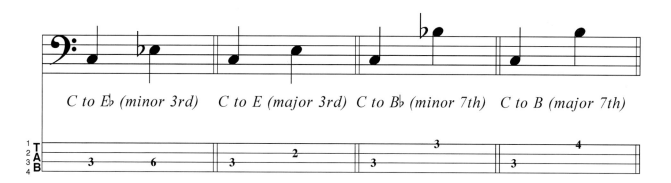

C to E♭ (minor 3rd)   C to E (major 3rd)   C to B♭ (minor 7th)   C to B (major 7th)

GRADE FIVE

a) Repetition of rhythms

The examiner will twice tap or play on a single note a four bar rhythm in ³⁄₄ ⁴⁄₄ or ⁶⁄₈ time. This will contain no note value shorter than a 16th note (semiquaver).

The candidate should then attempt to reproduce this rhythm by either clapping or playing. Some examples of the type of rhythm are given below.

b) Repetition of phrases

The phrase given at this grade will consist of notes within a range of one octave taken from a scale listed for Grade Five in Section 1 of this handbook – the candidate will be told which scale is to be used, and the tonic note will be played. The phrase will start either on the tonic or 5th note and will consist of 2 quarter notes (crotchets) and 4 eighth notes (quavers). Some examples of the type of phrases are shown below.

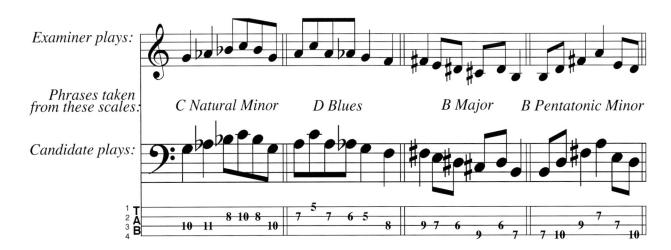

c) Beating of time

The examiner will twice play a four bar phrase in ³⁄₄ or ⁶⁄₈ time. The phrase will *not* begin on the first beat of the bar. After the first playing the candidate should identify the time signature.

During the second playing the candidate should tap or clap the main pulse, accenting the first beat of the bar. An example is given below.

Examiner plays:

Candidate taps:

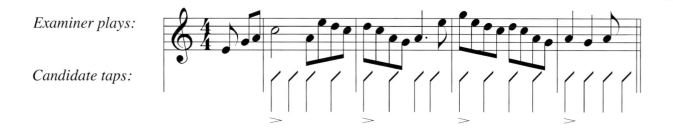

d) Harmony tests

The examiner will play two chords of the same nature and the candidate will be asked to identify the type of chord played. The chord types will be selected from the following list:

Minor 6th
Minor 7th
Sus 4th
Major 6th
Major 7th
Dominant 7th

e) Pitch tests

The examiner will play the tonic note of a major scale together with another note from the scale simultaneously. The key note will be stated. The candidate should identify the interval between the tonic note and the higher note. An example in the key of G is given below:

Although the two notes will be played together, the candidate may find it easier to identify the interval by trying to separate the two notes, singing from the lower to the higher note.

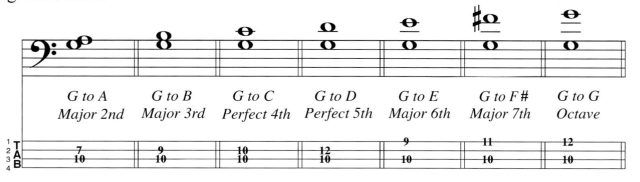

G to A	G to B	G to C	G to D	G to E	G to F♯	G to G
Major 2nd	Major 3rd	Perfect 4th	Perfect 5th	Major 6th	Major 7th	Octave

Conclusion

Examination tips

1. Many of the musical examples given in this handbook may be presented in different keys during the examination. Practising in a range of keys should be considered as essential examination preparation.

2. In the final weeks leading up to the examination practice should focus on weak areas, but do not neglect the main 'Bass Patterns' and 'Performance' sections as these carry the majority of the marks.

3. During the examination, the examiner's numerous questions and tests may seem daunting at first, but these are never designed to 'catch you out'. The breadth of the questions and tests are purely aimed at allowing you the opportunity to display the range and depth of the musical abilities and knowledge that you have developed. Although, as well as complimenting your achievements, the examiner will offer written advice on any areas in which you need to devote more study.

4. During the examination, the examiner will need to make written notes about your performance. This enables the examiner to compile a helpful examination report, which will be forwarded to you after the examination. So do not be put off if you see the examiner 'reach for a pen' – it does not necessarily mean that an error has been noted, it is just as likely that the examiner is noting a positive comment about some aspect of the performance.

5. Try to dispel any nerves by viewing the examination not as a daunting test, but rather as a positive opportunity to demonstrate your musical skills and talents, and to have these formally recognised and rewarded.

Entering for the examination

After studying this handbook, you may wish to enter for one of the examinations. Please ensure you are familiar with the general regulations and current requirements by reading the current Examination Syllabus and the Bass Guitar Exam Information Booklet – both downloadable from www.RGT.org

UK candidates may enter and pay for the examinations online via the RGT website, www.RGT.org, using the unique entry codes printed below *or* by using the entry forms in the back of this book.

To enter online visit **www.RGT.org** where entry fees can be paid by credit or debit card. In order to enter online you will need to input your unique and confidential examination entry code for the appropriate grade:

Grade Three Online Entry Code: BC-9931-BZ

Grade Four Online Entry Code: BD-7960-BA

Grade Five Online Entry Code: BE-7986-BB

Keep these codes confidential, as each one can only be used once.

Overseas candidates cannot enter for examinations online and should use the entry forms within this book.

Registry of Guitar Tutors
Registry Mews, 11 to 13 Wilton Road,
Bexhill, East Sussex, TN40 1HY

Tel: 01424 22 22 22   Fax: 01424 21 32 21

Email: office@RGT.org

Bass players – go surfing ...

... the Registry of Guitar Tutors' recommended website for bass guitar books and educational material

RGT
Registry of Guitar Tutors
The Specialists in Guitar Education

EXAMINATION ENTRY FORM
BASS GUITAR
GRADE THREE

ONLINE ENTRY – AVAILABLE FOR UK CANDIDATES ONLY

For **UK candidates**, entries and payments can be made online at www.RGT.org, using your unique and confidential examination entry code shown on page 57 of this book.

You will be able to pay the entry fee by credit or debit card at a secure payment page on the RGT website.

Once you have entered online, you should sign this form overleaf. **You must bring this signed form to your exam and hand it to the examiner in order to be admitted to the exam room.**

If NOT entering online, please complete BOTH sides of this form and return to the address overleaf.

SESSION (Spring/Summer/Winter): _____ YEAR: _____

Dates/times NOT available: _____

Note: Only name *specific* dates (and times on those dates) when it would be *absolutely impossible* for you to attend due to important prior commitments (such as pre-booked overseas travel) which cannot be cancelled. We will then endeavour to avoid scheduling an exam session in your area on those dates. In fairness to all other candidates in your area, **only list dates on which it would be impossible for you to attend.** An entry form that blocks out unreasonable periods may be returned. (Exams may be held on any day of the week including, but not exclusively, weekends. Exams may be held within or outside of the school term.)

Candidate Details: *Please write as clearly as possible using BLOCK CAPITALS*

Candidate Name (as to appear on certificate): _____

Address: _____

_____ Postcode: _____

Tel. No. (day): _____ (mobile): _____

IMPORTANT: Please take care to write your email address below *as clearly as possible* as your exam entry acknowledgement and your exam appointment details will be sent to this email address. Only provide an email address that is in regular monitored use.

Email:_____

Where an email address is provided your exam correspondence will be sent by email only, and not by post. This will ensure your exam correspondence will reach you sooner.

Teacher Details (if applicable)

Teacher Name (as to appear on certificate): _____

RGT Tutor Code (if applicable):_____

Address: _____

_____ Postcode: _____

Tel. No. (day): _____ (mobile): _____

Email:_____

BASS GUITAR – RGT Official Entry Form

The standard LCM entry form is NOT valid for Bass Guitar exam entries.
Entry to the examination is only possible via this original form.
Photocopies of this form will not be accepted under any circumstances.

- Completion of this entry form is an agreement to comply with the current syllabus requirements and conditions of entry published at www.RGT.org. Where candidates are entered for examinations by a teacher, parent or guardian that person hereby takes responsibility that the candidate is entered in accordance with the current syllabus requirements and conditions of entry.

- If you are being taught by an *RGT registered* tutor, please hand this completed form to your tutor and request him/her to administer the entry on your behalf.

- For candidates with special needs, a letter giving details should be attached.

Examination Fee: £_____   Late Entry Fee (if applicable): £_____

Total amount submitted: £_____

Cheques or postal orders should be made payable to Registry of Guitar Tutors.

Details of conditions of entry, entry deadlines and examination fees are obtainable from the RGT website: www.RGT.org

Once an entry has been accepted, entry fees cannot be refunded.

CANDIDATE INFORMATION (UK Candidates only)

In order to meet our obligations in monitoring the implementation of equal opportunities policies, UK candidates are required to supply the information requested below. The information provided will in no way whatsoever influence the marks awarded during the examination.

Date of birth: _____ Age: _____ Gender – please circle: <u>male / female</u>

Ethnicity (please enter 2 digit code from chart below): _____ Signed: _____

ETHNIC ORIGIN CLASSIFICATIONS (If you prefer not to say, write '17' in the space above.)

White: <u>**01** British</u>   **02** Irish   **03** Other white background

Mixed: <u>**04** White & black Caribbean</u>   **05** White & black African   **06** White & Asian   **07** Other mixed background

Asian or Asian British: **08** Indian   **09** Pakistani   **10** Bangladeshi   **11** Other Asian background

Black or Black British: <u>**12** Caribbean</u>   **13** African   **14** Other black background

Chinese or Other Ethnic Group: <u>**15** Chinese</u>   **16** Other   **17** Prefer not to say

I understand and accept the current syllabus regulations and conditions of entry for this examination as specified on the RGT website.

Signed by candidate (if aged 18 or over) _____ Date _____

If candidate is under 18, this form should be signed by a parent/guardian/teacher (circle which applies):

Signed _____ Name_____ Date_____

UK ENTRIES

See overleaf for details of how to enter online OR return this form to:
Registry of Guitar Tutors, Registry Mews, 11 to 13 Wilton Road, Bexhill-on-Sea, E. Sussex, TN40 1HY
(If you have submitted your entry online do NOT post this form, instead you need to sign it above and hand it to the examiner on the day of your exam.)
To contact the RGT office telephone 01424 222222 or Email office@RGT.org

NON-UK ENTRIES

To locate the address within your country that entry forms should be sent to, and to view exam fees in your currency, visit the RGT website **www.RGT.org** and navigate to the 'RGT Worldwide' section.

RGT
Registry of Guitar Tutors

EXAMINATION ENTRY FORM
BASS GUITAR
GRADE FOUR

ONLINE ENTRY – AVAILABLE FOR UK CANDIDATES ONLY

For **UK candidates**, entries and payments can be made online at www.RGT.org, using your unique and confidential examination entry code shown on page 57 of this book.

You will be able to pay the entry fee by credit or debit card at a secure payment page on the RGT website.

Once you have entered online, you should sign this form overleaf. **You must bring this signed form to your exam and hand it to the examiner in order to be admitted to the exam room.**

If NOT entering online, please complete BOTH sides of this form and return to the address overleaf.

SESSION (Spring/Summer/Winter): _____ YEAR: _____

Dates/times NOT available: _____

Note: Only name *specific* dates (and times on those dates) when it would be <u>absolutely impossible</u> for you to attend due to important prior commitments (such as pre-booked overseas travel) which cannot be cancelled. We will then endeavour to avoid scheduling an exam session in your area on those dates. In fairness to all other candidates in your area, **only list dates on which it would be impossible for you to attend.** An entry form that blocks out unreasonable periods may be returned. (Exams may be held on any day of the week including, but not exclusively, weekends. Exams may be held within or outside of the school term.)

Candidate Details: *Please write as clearly as possible using BLOCK CAPITALS*

Candidate Name (as to appear on certificate): _____

Address: _____

_____ Postcode: _____

Tel. No. (day): _____ (mobile): _____

IMPORTANT: Please take care to write your email address below *as clearly as possible* as your exam entry acknowledgement and your exam appointment details will be sent to this email address. Only provide an email address that is in regular monitored use.

Email:_____
Where an email address is provided your exam correspondence will be sent by email only, and not by post. This will ensure your exam correspondence will reach you sooner.

Teacher Details *(if applicable)*

Teacher Name (as to appear on certificate): _____

RGT Tutor Code (if applicable):_____

Address: _____

_____ Postcode: _____

Tel. No. (day): _____ (mobile): _____

Email:_____

BASS GUITAR – RGT Official Entry Form

The standard LCM entry form is NOT valid for Bass Guitar exam entries.
Entry to the examination is only possible via this original form.
Photocopies of this form will not be accepted under any circumstances.

- Completion of this entry form is an agreement to comply with the current syllabus requirements and conditions of entry published at www.RGT.org. Where candidates are entered for examinations by a teacher, parent or guardian that person hereby takes responsibility that the candidate is entered in accordance with the current syllabus requirements and conditions of entry.

- If you are being taught by an *RGT registered* tutor, please hand this completed form to your tutor and request him/her to administer the entry on your behalf.

- For candidates with special needs, a letter giving details should be attached.

Examination Fee: £_____   Late Entry Fee (if applicable): £_____

Total amount submitted: £_____

Cheques or postal orders should be made payable to Registry of Guitar Tutors.

Details of conditions of entry, entry deadlines and examination fees are obtainable from the RGT website: www.RGT.org

Once an entry has been accepted, entry fees cannot be refunded.

CANDIDATE INFORMATION (UK Candidates only)

In order to meet our obligations in monitoring the implementation of equal opportunities policies, UK candidates are required to supply the information requested below. The information provided will in no way whatsoever influence the marks awarded during the examination.

Date of birth: _____ Age: _____ Gender – please circle: <u>male / female</u>

Ethnicity (please enter 2 digit code from chart below): _____ Signed: _____

ETHNIC ORIGIN CLASSIFICATIONS (If you prefer not to say, write '17' in the space above.)

White: **<u>01</u> British**   **<u>02</u> Irish**   **<u>03</u> Other white background**

Mixed: **<u>04</u> White & black Caribbean**   **<u>05</u> White & black African**   **<u>06</u> White & Asian**   **<u>07</u> Other mixed background**

Asian or Asian British: **<u>08</u> Indian**   **<u>09</u> Pakistani**   **<u>10</u> Bangladeshi**   **<u>11</u> Other Asian background**

Black or Black British: **<u>12</u> Caribbean**   **<u>13</u> African**   **<u>14</u> Other black background**

Chinese or Other Ethnic Group: **<u>15</u> Chinese**   **<u>16</u> Other**   **<u>17</u> Prefer not to say**

I understand and accept the current syllabus regulations and conditions of entry for this examination as specified on the RGT website.

Signed by candidate (if aged 18 or over) _____ Date _____

If candidate is under 18, this form should be signed by a parent/guardian/teacher (circle which applies):

Signed _____ Name_____ Date_____

UK ENTRIES

See overleaf for details of how to enter online OR return this form to:
Registry of Guitar Tutors, Registry Mews, 11 to 13 Wilton Road, Bexhill-on-Sea, E. Sussex, TN40 1HY
(If you have submitted your entry online do NOT post this form, instead you need to sign it above and hand it to the examiner on the day of your exam.)
To contact the RGT office telephone 01424 222222 or Email office@RGT.org

NON-UK ENTRIES

To locate the address within your country that entry forms should be sent to, and to view exam fees in your currency, visit the RGT website **www.RGT.org** and navigate to the 'RGT Worldwide' section.

RGT
Registry of Guitar Tutors

EXAMINATION ENTRY FORM
BASS GUITAR
GRADE FIVE

ONLINE ENTRY – AVAILABLE FOR UK CANDIDATES ONLY

For **UK candidates**, entries and payments can be made online at www.RGT.org, using your unique and confidential examination entry code shown on page 57 of this book.

You will be able to pay the entry fee by credit or debit card at a secure payment page on the RGT website.

Once you have entered online, you should sign this form overleaf. **You must bring this signed form to your exam and hand it to the examiner in order to be admitted to the exam room.**

If NOT entering online, please complete BOTH sides of this form and return to the address overleaf.

SESSION (Spring/Summer/Winter): _____ YEAR: _____

Dates/times NOT available: _____

Note: Only name *specific* dates (and times on those dates) when it would be _absolutely impossible_ for you to attend due to important prior commitments (such as pre-booked overseas travel) which cannot be cancelled. We will then endeavour to avoid scheduling an exam session in your area on those dates. In fairness to all other candidates in your area, **only list dates on which it would be impossible for you to attend.** An entry form that blocks out unreasonable periods may be returned. (Exams may be held on any day of the week including, but not exclusively, weekends. Exams may be held within or outside of the school term.)

Candidate Details: *Please write as clearly as possible using BLOCK CAPITALS*

Candidate Name (as to appear on certificate): _____

Address: _____

_____ Postcode: _____

Tel. No. (day): _____ (mobile): _____

IMPORTANT: Please take care to write your email address below *as clearly as possible* as your exam entry acknowledgement and your exam appointment details will be sent to this email address. Only provide an email address that is in regular monitored use.

Email: _____
Where an email address is provided your exam correspondence will be sent by email only, and not by post. This will ensure your exam correspondence will reach you sooner.

Teacher Details *(if applicable)*

Teacher Name (as to appear on certificate): _____

RGT Tutor Code (if applicable): _____

Address: _____

_____ Postcode: _____

Tel. No. (day): _____ (mobile): _____

Email: _____

BASS GUITAR – RGT Official Entry Form

- Completion of this entry form is an agreement to comply with the current syllabus requirements and conditions of entry published at www.RGT.org. Where candidates are entered for examinations by a teacher, parent or guardian that person hereby takes responsibility that the candidate is entered in accordance with the current syllabus requirements and conditions of entry.

- If you are being taught by an *RGT registered* tutor, please hand this completed form to your tutor and request him/her to administer the entry on your behalf.

- For candidates with special needs, a letter giving details should be attached.

Examination Fee: £_____   Late Entry Fee (if applicable): £_____

Total amount submitted: £_____

Cheques or postal orders should be made payable to Registry of Guitar Tutors

Details of conditions of entry, entry deadlines and examination fees are obtainable from the RGT website: www.RGT.org

Once an entry has been accepted, entry fees cannot be refunded.

CANDIDATE INFORMATION (UK Candidates only)

In order to meet our obligations in monitoring the implementation of equal opportunities policies, UK candidates are required to supply the information requested below. The information provided will in no way whatsoever influence the marks awarded during the examination.

Date of birth: _____ Age: _____ Gender – please circle: male / female

Ethnicity (please enter 2 digit code from chart below): _____ Signed: _____

ETHNIC ORIGIN CLASSIFICATIONS (If you prefer not to say, write '17' in the space above.)

White: **01 British**   **02 Irish**   **03 Other white background**

Mixed: **04 White & black Caribbean**   **05 White & black African**   **06 White & Asian**   **07 Other mixed background**

Asian or Asian British: **08 Indian**   **09 Pakistani**   **10 Bangladeshi**   **11 Other Asian background**

Black or Black British: **12 Caribbean**   **13 African**   **14 Other black background**

Chinese or Other Ethnic Group: **15 Chinese**   **16 Other**   **17 Prefer not to say**

I understand and accept the current syllabus regulations and conditions of entry for this examination as specified on the RGT website.

Signed by candidate (if aged 18 or over) _____ Date _____

If candidate is under 18, this form should be signed by a parent/guardian/teacher (circle which applies):

Signed _____ Name_____ Date_____

UK ENTRIES

See overleaf for details of how to enter online OR return this form to:
Registry of Guitar Tutors, Registry Mews, 11 to 13 Wilton Road, Bexhill-on-Sea, E. Sussex, TN40 1HY
(If you have submitted your entry online do NOT post this form, instead you need to sign it above and hand it to the examiner on the day of your exam.)
To contact the RGT office telephone 01424 222222 or Email office@RGT.org

NON-UK ENTRIES

To locate the address within your country that entry forms should be sent to, and to view exam fees in your currency, visit the RGT website **www.RGT.org** and navigate to the 'RGT Worldwide' section.